# MADELEINES

## FOR MATT AND LANEY

Copyright © 2014 by Barbara Feldman Morse

Photography copyright © 2014 by Steve Legato

All rights reserved. No part of this book may be reproduced in any form without written permission from the publisher.

Library of Congress Cataloging in Publication Number: 2013957087

ISBN: 978-1-59474-740-3

Printed in China

Designed by Amanda Richmond

Production management by John J. McGurk

Prop styling by Mariellen Melker

Quirk Books
215 Church St.
Philadelphia, PA 19106
quirkbooks.com
10 9 8 7 6 5 4 3 2

# MADELEINES

## ELEGANT FRENCH TEA CAKES TO BAKE AND SHARE

BY BARBARA FELDMAN MORSE

QUIRK
BOOKS

# CONTENTS

## CH 3
# DARK AND DELUXE CHOCOLATE MADELEINES ...76

## CH 4
# FRUIT AND NUTS ...98

## CH 5
## SAVORY AND APPETIZER ...116

## CH 6
## INDULGENT MADELEINES ...130

# INTRODUCTION

**I GREW UP ON THE SOUTH SHORE OF BOSTON, WHICH MEANT SPENDING SUMMERS** along the Atlantic Ocean. Some of my earliest memories are of collecting scallop shells with my sister and brother while our mother and grandmother cooked chowders and baked stuffed clams back at the house. When it was time to leave our sandy escape each September, my favorite shells always came along–the perfect portable reminder of all the beauty and joy the beach held.

My love for shells only grew as I got older. I'll always be a collector of these seaside souvenirs, opting to hunt for the prettiest shells instead of plopping in a beach chair any day. So discovering my first madeleine pan in a small baking shop in San Francisco was a "eureka!" moment. Time seemed to stand still while I thought of making little cakelets shaped like the summertime shells I loved collecting so much.

As soon as I brought those pans home to my tiny studio apartment, I started searching for madeleine recipes. I tried as many as I could find–which wasn't very many in the pre-Internet 1970s. Imagine how let down I was when I discovered that madeleines were all plain vanilla, kind of dry, and fairly bland. Yet I sensed they had potential, so I started testing different flavors, textures, and techniques. The recipes in this book are the result of the many years of experimentation that followed.

These recipes will delight you in so many ways. Not only will you learn how to bake madeleines that are scrumptious and full of unexpected flavors, you'll also master a foolproof method that's incredibly quick and easy. In fact, making the recipes in this book is such a cinch that I'm willing to bet you'll find yourself baking batches all the time–for birthday parties or potlucks, when unexpected guests arrive at your door, or even when you're home alone on a weekend night. I've even been known to whip some up at a moment's notice for a posse of teenage girls craving a midnight sleepover snack.

These recipes will make you look and feel like a whiz in the kitchen no matter your previous baking experience or skills. Their simplicity, as well as my time-saving one-bowl method, is what inspired me to write this book. I hope you'll find my inventive combinations of flavors and ingredients so easy and rewarding that you'll be inspired to try your own variations. Nothing would make me happier than to have new and experienced bakers alike using my recipes as a starting point for dozens of delicious seashell-shaped creations.

So go ahead–get yourself some madeleine pans and break out your mixing bowl! You are about to experience the joy of baking a quintessential dessert without the stress usually associated with French cooking. Marcel Proust may have put madeleines on the map when he waxed poetic about the "exquisite pleasure that invaded [his] senses," but you're about to put these little French tea cakes into the mouths of everyone you know. Move over, cupcakes and cronuts–it's time for the madeleine!

# FOR THE LOVE
## OF MADELEINES

**FROM NOTES ON THE PERFECT INGREDIENTS** AND
indispensable equipment to the secrets I've learned from
years of baking, here's everything you need to know to
make madeleines your special signature treat.

*REMEMB*
Duke alone wh
in the house,
saw no furth
the people.
A min
anyone
ask m
be
con
b

# A Brief History

WHAT, EXACTLY, IS A MADELEINE? TRADITIONALLY MADELEINES ARE DESCRIBED AS "small, shell-shaped cakes made of flour, eggs, sugar, and butter and baked in molds." Stories vary about how and when these adorable French tea cakes were born, but most experts agree that they're named after Madeleine Paulmier, a pastry chef from Commercy, a town in the Lorraine region of France. Some claim that Paulmier created the sweet treat in the nineteenth century, but legend has it that she baked them as early as the eighteenth century for Stanislaw Lezczynski, the Duke of Lorraine, and his son-in-law Louis XV. According to that story, the French king liked the sponge cakes so much that he named them after her.

Regardless of when they first came out of an oven or how they got their name, the recipe quickly spread. These tasty tea cakes became a part of French culture and even literature. The madeleine's place in literary history was assured thanks to Marcel Proust, the writer, essayist, and critic best known for his autobiographical novel, *À la recherche du temps perdu*, published in seven parts from 1913 to 1927. (The book was translated into English as *In Search of Lost Time*, also known as *Remembrance of Things Past*.) Proust used examples to contrast voluntary memories–those retrieved by "intelligence" and produced by making a conscious effort to remember people or places–with involuntary memories, which, according to Proust's narrator, come naturally when the moment one remembers is magical.

To explain the latter, Proust describes biting into a childhood snack. In the now famous "episode of the madeleine," he writes:

*No sooner had the warm liquid mixed with the crumbs touched my palate than a shudder ran through me and I stopped, intent upon the extraordinary thing that was happening to me. An exquisite pleasure had invaded my senses, something isolated, detached, with no suggestion of its origin. And at once the vicissitudes of life had become indifferent to me, its disasters innocuous, its brevity illusory–this new sensation having had on me the effect which love has of filling me with a precious essence; or rather this essence was not in me it was me. ... Whence did it come? What did it mean? How could I seize and apprehend it? ... And suddenly the memory revealed itself. The taste was that of the little piece of madeleine which on Sunday mornings at Combray (because on those mornings I did not go out before mass), when I went to say good morning to her in her bedroom, my aunt Léonie used to give me, dipping it first in her own cup of tea or tisane. The sight of the little madeleine had recalled nothing to my mind before I tasted it. And all from my cup of tea.*

We'll never know the exact recipe for the madeleine so magical that it prompted involuntary memories for dear Monsieur Proust. But one thing I am sure of is that the recipes in this book are so scrumptious, they will prompt you to make your own sweet memories for years to come.

# Secrets to Baking Magical Madeleines

**I'VE HAD PLENTY OF YEARS OF TRIAL AND ERROR, WHICH IS WHY I WANT TO SHARE** all the tips and tricks I've learned along the way. Follow this advice and your madeleines will be perfect, starting with the very first batch.

## GET YOUR MISE EN PLACE IN PLACE

*Mise en place* (pronounced *meez-ahn-plahss*) is a French term that translates literally as "set in place." Chefs around the world use this phrase to describe the process of organizing what you need for a recipe before you start to cook or bake.

For madeleines, you'll need to collect the pans, bowls, whisks, ingredients, and other utensils or equipment called for in the recipe. Next, prepare any ingredients according to the descriptions in the list–for example, toast nuts, chop and weigh chocolate, grate a lemon, and so on. Getting your mise en place in order before you delve into any recipe is the best way to avoid forgetting an ingredient or a part of the process. The result is a smoother, more enjoyable baking experience.

*From left to right: Fine-mesh sieve, grater, French whisk, ice cream scoops, and offset spatula.*

## INGREDIENTS

WHEN IT COMES TO THE STUFF THAT GREAT MADELEINES ARE MADE OF, FRESH IS always best. Extracts and seasonings lose their potency over time; juicing a lemon on the spot will mean a bolder citrus flavor than would be had from bottled lemon juice. In my opinion, it is much better to hold off on baking until you can replace a not-so-fresh ingredient with one of better quality.

The good news is that all the recipes in this book can be made with readily available ingredients, most of which you probably already have in your kitchen. Here's what to keep on hand, as well as "add-in" items that will allow you to create endless variations.

### BUTTER

There is no substitute for the flavor and texture of real butter in baked goods. You'll need unsalted butter for the sweet madeleines and either salted or unsalted for the savory varieties. In a pinch, however, you can use either in all the recipes. Just be sure to remove butter from the refrigerator 30 to 60 minutes before baking if the recipe calls for whipping it with the sugar. You won't get that "light and fluffy" consistency if you trying to whip butter that's chilled.

### BAKING SPRAY

Coating your pans with cooking spray– either regular spray or baking spray with flour–will help ensure that your madeleines fall out of their molds. The spray with flour seems to create a slightly more golden brown madeleine, so that is what I use. If you don't have spray, coat the molds with melted butter.

### SUGARS

Most of the recipes in this book call for white granulated sugar. A few require dark brown sugar, but substituting light brown sugar is fine. (You get a more pronounced flavor from the molasses in the dark variety.) Confectioners' sugar lightly sifted over cooled madeleines creates a pretty finish. Glittery and colored sanding sugars and crystals can dress up plain madeleines easily and quickly, if that's what you desire. I sprinkle decorating sugars onto the batter before baking.

## EGGS

You'll want to use either white or brown large eggs, the most common size available in the United States. The U.S. Department of Agriculture calculates egg size by weight per dozen. Large eggs, which are called for in all the recipes here, weigh in at more than 2 ounces each.

## FLOURS

Unbleached all-purpose flour is what I used to develop the recipes in this book. Commercial gluten-free flour mixes can be substituted cup for cup in place of all-purpose flour and will lead to an equally delectable, though slightly grittier, madeleine.

## BAKING POWDER

Double-acting baking powder is a leavening agent that helps madeleines rise to a medium bump or higher, depending on the amount the recipe calls for. Replace your baking powder every six months, which is when it loses its efficacy. Traditional madeleines do not call for baking powder; whisking for several minutes aerates the batter so that the heat of the oven helps the cakes rise.

## VANILLA AND OTHER EXTRACTS

There is no substitute for pure extract, so be sure that the ones you buy don't say "imitation" or "flavoring." The most common extract you'll use in these recipes is vanilla. Vanilla bean paste may be substituted teaspoon for teaspoon for pure vanilla extract; it supplies those wonderful specks that look so pretty in baked goods. See "Resources" (page 168) for good sources of vanilla.

Two other extracts to consider whisking into your madeleine batter are orange blossom water and rosewater. Either substitute them for the vanilla or use half orange blossom or rosewater and half vanilla.

## CHOCOLATE AND COCOA POWDER

The recipes in this book call for a range of chocolates, from unsweetened and extra-bittersweet to semisweet, milk chocolate, and white chocolate varieties. You'll likely find an array of chocolates at your grocery store amid an ever-expanding selection of chips, chunks, and slabs. My advice is to purchase the best-quality chocolate you can afford.

Some of the recipes in this book also call for cocoa powder. You'll find two types at the grocery store, both of which are unsweetened. Dutch-processed cocoa powder is darker and treated with an alkali to neutralize its acidity. Familiar brands include Droste, Valrhona, Whole Foods Bulk cocoa, and Hershey's Special Dark. It's fine to substitute natural cocoa powder for Dutch-processed in most cases, but not the other way around. I like to use Dutch-processed cocoa powder when I want a deep, rich color and flavor. I also use it for sifting over chocolate madeleines as a simple finish before serving. Natural, unsweetened cocoa powder, such as Hershey's Cocoa, is used when baking soda (an alkali) is called for. The baking soda causes the leavening to occur when the batter is placed in the hot oven because the acidity hasn't been tempered, as in Dutch-processed cocoa.

## NUTS

The crunchy texture and varied flavors of nuts are fantastic additions to madeleines. Toasting is the first step to achieving superior taste–it intensifies a nut's flavor and transforms the texture from buttery to crunchy. To toast nuts, place them in a single layer on a baking sheet and bake at 300°F for 15 to 20 minutes. Every 5 minutes or so, stir with a spatula to ensure even browning.

# EQUIPMENT

The right tools will ensure perfect madeleines every time. Here's a list of the necessary baking equipment, plus a few luxuries that will make you feel like a professional baker.

## MADELEINE PANS

To bake true madeleines, you need proper molds. The beauty of these special pans is that they come in all different shapes, sizes, and materials. From mini-madeleine pans with nonstick coating to round shell molds in heavy-gauge tinned steel, a range is available at home goods and kitchen supply stores, in baking shops and catalogues, and through many online retailers.

I prefer nonstick pans, which I recommend for both seasoned and novice bakers alike. The nontoxic, nonstick coating allows the madeleines to slip out easily after they're baked, and washing will be easy and fast. Just remember that nonstick pans still need to be buttered or sprayed with baking spray. Careful pan preparation is key to ensuring successful madeleines.

---

## PAN PREP

A fast and reliable method for preparing pans of all kinds—including nonstick types—is to coat the surface lightly with a canned cooking spray. I do this over the sink so it's easier to clean the excess spray. You can also prep pans with butter. Melt 3 to 4 tablespoons of butter in a small bowl; then use a pastry brush to coat all the nooks and flutes of the shell molds. However you decide to prep your pans, an even coat is crucial for the quick and easy release of the madeleines. Both methods are simple and effective.

---

## BOWLS

Any medium-size microwave-safe bowl will work just fine when making all the recipes in this book. For my quick and easy madeleine method, I recommend using a 2-quart glass bowl or measuring cup (such as Pyrex brand). In addition to being microwave safe, the bowl should have a wide bottom, which prevents tipping when you're whisking and stirring. A handle is also useful, allowing you to pour batter directly into the molds. You can also use a 1-quart (4-cup) bowl, but the 2-quart (8-cup) size gives you a little more room to whisk. I also love a 2-quart clear glass bowl with a cover; the cover comes in handy when you want to make the batter ahead and chill it overnight.

## WHISKS

French-style whisks are my favorite for making madeleines. They are stainless steel and measure about 8 inches long and only $1^1/_2$ inches at the widest point. The stiffness and narrower width allow thorough mixing at the bottom of the bowl.

## SPATULAS

I frequently mention using a small offset spatula. These are useful for many tasks: to glaze, blend melted chocolate, apply decorations, and gently nudge madeleines out of their shells. Rubber spatulas are available in many sizes and shapes (and even pretty colors). I use them for folding, mixing, blending, and scraping every last bit of batter out of a bowl. I prefer silicone spatulas, which are able to take the heat when stirring ingredients in a double boiler.

## ICE CREAM SCOOP

I use a spring-action scoop to transfer batter into molds. I find the scoop is neater and faster than a spoon, and it helps create madeleines of uniform size. Most often I use a $1^1/_2$-inch scoop, plus a smaller size for mini madeleines.

## COOLING RACKS

You'll need to set hot pans on racks and then place the madeleines on those same racks to cool. I prefer large heavyweight racks. They make it easy to move an entire batch of madeleines from the kitchen counter to the table, where you've laid out your decorations.

## MEASURING CUPS AND SPOONS

One surefire way to ensure baking success is to accurately measure ingredients. Measure dry ingredients in good-quality metal measuring cups and spoons; you'll need $^1/_4$ cup, $^1/_3$ cup, $^1/_2$ cup, and 1

cup. Measuring spoons are available in increments of $^1/_4$ teaspoon, $^1/_2$ teaspoon, 1 teaspoon, and 1 tablespoon.

Liquids should be measured in clear glass measuring cups that have measurements printed on the side. It's best to fill them on a flat surface and then observe the measurement at eye level to be sure it's correct.

## STAND AND HAND MIXERS

I have owned several heavy-duty stand mixers. They are remarkably dependable, worth the investment (they last years!), and crucial when it comes to a few of the recipes in this book. If you don't own one, a handheld mixer will work in its place, because the batter for the madeleines is relatively light and the quantities are small. Another bonus of the handheld mixer: it fits easily into the 2-quart microwavable bowl you're already using for these recipes, which means one less thing to wash.

So, when should you use a stand or hand mixer versus whisking by hand? Using the mixer adds more air into the batter than hand-mixing does, resulting in a madeleine with a consistency that's more like cake than a cookie. Therefore, you should use a stand or hand mixer when you want a finer-grain madeleine that has a texture similar to pound or sponge cake.

## ZESTERS OR MICROPLANES

Using a Microplane for freshly grated citrus zest will change your life! They work so much better than box graters, and you'll quickly discover that fresh zest is incomparable to dried when it comes to flavor. Microplanes also come in handy for serving. Freshly shaved chocolate, or even a sprinkle of grated lemon, orange, lime, or grapefruit rind, creates a gorgeous finish to a platter of fresh-from-the-oven madeleines.

## TIMER

A timer with a loud bell or buzzer will be the best reminder to check your madeleines. It's easy to become distracted when baking, so a reliable timer is handy for success.

## APRONS AND OVEN MITTS

Batters and glazes can splash and drip, so I always wear an apron to protect my clothes and to set the stage for baking. Oven mitts are essential, and I am fussy about the ones I buy. I prefer smaller sizes that are flexible, allowing me to grab pans more easily. I set them out during my *mise en place*. There's nothing more frustrating than searching for mitts at the precise moment the madeleines need to come out of the oven.

# How to Make Madeleines

THERE'S MORE THAN ONE METHOD TO BAKE MADELEINES. THE CLASSIC WAY CALLS for melting the butter separately, then folding it into a batter of egg, sugar, and flour. This method creates a pound-cake-like madeleine with the quintessential "hump" in the middle. My one-bowl method directs you to first melt the butter and sugar together. Then you whisk the eggs, flavoring, and flour into the same bowl for a quick batter that's ready to scoop, bake, and serve. Both methods work well, so feel free to experiment and see which one you like best.

# THE CLASSIC METHOD

The classic batter for madeleines is a genoise mixture. Named after the Italian city of Genoa, genoise is a foamlike cake that's often used for wedding cakes, sheet cakes, ladyfingers, and petits fours, as well as traditional madeleines. The leavening happens as a result of air being whipped into the egg–sugar mixture, combined with the heat of the oven, rather than through chemical agents such as baking powder or baking soda. The resulting madeleines tend to look like small, plump pound cakes.

**1.** Place the butter in a 2-quart microwavable bowl. Microwave on low power for 1 to 2 minutes. Whisk to blend and return to the microwave for 15-second intervals until the butter is fully melted. Let cool.

**2.** Combine the eggs and sugar and warm gently.

**3.** Beat the egg and sugar mixture until thick and foamy. I suggest using a handheld or stand mixer, which will save time.

**4.** Add the flour and flavorings, if using.

**5.** Fold in the melted butter.

**6.** Scoop the batter evenly into prepared pans.

**7.** Bake until madeleines puff up and no shiny spots remain in the centers. Remove the pans from the oven, let cool on a wire rack for 2 to 3 minutes, and then carefully remove the madeleines using a small offset spatula.

# THE ONE-BOWL METHOD

I've developed a nontraditional method that yields equally delicious and successful results. This shortcut was born from the need to speed things up when I was operating a baking business. I found it to be the fastest and simplest way to make hundreds of madeleines that turned out just as tender and lovely as the ones I made using the classic method. Here's how to do it.

MADELEINES

**1.** Place the room-temperature butter (cut into tablespoon-size pieces), sugar, and chopped chocolate (if using) in a 2-quart microwavable bowl.

**2.** Microwave on low power for 1 to 2 minutes. Whisk to blend and then return to the microwave for 15-second intervals until the butter is fully melted.

**3.** Whisk the mixture until it is smooth and the batter falls from the whisk in ribbons. You may also use a hand mixer, which will create a fluffier mixture more quickly.

**4.** Add the eggs (which should be room temperature) one at a time, whisking vigorously until evenly blended. Whisk for another minute or two to incorporate more air into the batter, which results in a finer crumb.

**5.** Add any flavorings, extracts, citrus peel, herbs, spices, or liqueurs to the batter. Whisk to blend completely.

**6.** Stir in the flour just until it disappears into the batter.

**7.** Scoop the batter evenly into the prepared pans.

**8.** Bake until the madeleines puff up and no shiny spots remain in the centers. Remove pans from the oven, let cool on a wire rack for 2 to 3 minutes, and then carefully remove the madeleines using a small offset spatula.

# FIVE TIPS FOR CREATING
# PERFECT MADELEINES

**I'VE BEEN BAKING FOR MORE THAN 30 YEARS, AND I'VE HAD MY FAIR SHARE OF FLOPS** even though I'm a professional baker. The most important advice I can offer as you embark on making madeleines is just to have fun. These recipes will help you learn to trust your senses, hit your stride, and relax. Here are five essential tips for creating perfect madeleines each and every time.

1. Use a timer as a guide. It will remind you to check on the madeleines and see how they look, but keep in mind that baking times vary. Those given in the recipes are a range and will depend on your oven and your location. If the batter seems unbaked, wait another minute or two, even if the recipe indicates doneness after a specific number of minutes.

2. Whisk the ingredients for 2 to 3 minutes. This step might not seem necessary, but it's important to whip air into the batter to get the fine crumb that the madeleine is known for.

3. Let the batter cool before you add the eggs. I know how tempting it is to keep charging ahead when the mixture comes out of the microwave, but if it's too hot, the eggs will scramble.

4. Use an ice cream scoop instead of a spoon to fill the shell molds. Scooping creates a more uniform size, which means that all the madeleines will finish baking at the same time. If some of the molds are filled more than others, the thin ones will bake more quickly than the plumper ones.

5. Place the pan on a wire cooling rack when it comes out of the oven. The madeleines need to sit for a minute or two before they're removed from their molds because at this stage they are very tender and may crumble. What's more, their super-soft spongelike quality means that whatever pattern is on your cooling racks will transfer onto the flat side of the still-warm madeleine.

# Simple Storage Solutions

FOR THE RARE OCCASION WHEN ALL OF YOUR MADELEINES DON'T DISAPPEAR IN A single sitting, you'll want to ensure they stay fresh for as long as possible. Madeleines will keep for 2 to 3 days if wrapped in an airtight container. Wrap them only after they've cooled completely, for steam will make them soggy. I also use zip-close baggies to store fresh madeleines or for freezing. Madeleines can be frozen for up to 2 months. Wrap them completely cooled in a freezer-safe container or zip-close bag, layering them between sheets of waxed paper. Defrost the madeleines at room temperature for 2 to 3 hours. You can even pop them briefly in the microwave before serving.

CH **1**

# NOT JUST PLAIN VANILLA

**THE DETAILS OF THE MADELEINE THAT MARCEL** Proust waxed poetic about don't exist, which means we're left to reverse-engineer the recipe that inspired such an "exquisite pleasure." Here's what we do know: We know Proust was a dunker. We know his madeleine was dry enough to crumble in his mouth. We know its flavor paired well with floral-tasting linden tea. Based on these clues, I'm willing to bet the recipe was similar to the classic French or vanilla madeleines you'll find here. And though these delicious (yet plain-ish) madeleines may have wowed Proust, plenty of other ingredients can enhance this iconic vanilla sponge cakelet, from cream cheese and poppy seeds to eggnog and Kahlúa.

*Classic French Madeleines (page 32)*

# ❧ CLASSIC FRENCH MADELEINES ❧

**I USED TO THINK THERE WAS NOTHING LIKE A FLAKY CROISSANT TO MAKE ME LONG** to live in France. Then I made these madeleines. The buttery, lemony flavor, combined with the gorgeous seashell shape–ridged on one side, smooth on the other–inspires daydreams of moving to one of Paris's *arrondissements*. And here's the best part: Although on this side of the pond a legitimate-tasting croissant is tough to find (let alone to bake!), these classic French madeleines are a cinch to make and taste divine. Serve them plain or dust them with confectioners' sugar to jazz them up *juste un petit peu*.

## YIELD: **24** MADELEINES

8 tbsp (1 stick) unsalted butter, plus 4 tbsp for pans (optional)

1 cup all-purpose flour

$^1/_2$ tsp baking powder

3 large eggs

$^2/_3$ cup granulated sugar

1 tsp vanilla bean paste or vanilla extract

$1^1/_2$ tsp freshly grated lemon zest

1. Place a rack in the center of the oven and preheat oven to 350°F. Coat two 12-shell pans with baking spray, or melt an additional 4 tablespoons butter and brush in each mold.

2. In a small bowl, whisk together flour and baking powder.

3. Place butter in another bowl and microwave on low power for 1 minute, or until melted. Allow to cool to room temperature.

4. Place eggs and sugar in a 2-quart glass bowl or measuring cup and beat with a hand or stand mixer on medium-high speed until mixture is light and fluffy, about 3 to 5 minutes.

5. Add vanilla and zest and continue beating for another minute or so. Fold in the flour mixture until just blended, then drizzle the cooled butter over the batter and incorporate completely.

6. Using a $1^1/_2$-inch-diameter scoop or a teaspoon, fill shell molds with batter until almost full. Gently press batter to distribute it evenly.

7. Bake for 10 to 12 minutes, until madeleines puff up and are golden brown.

8. Remove pans from oven and let cool on a wire rack for 2 to 3 minutes, then invert and tap madeleines onto the rack. You may also use a small offset spatula to remove each one individually. Let cool completely if planning to store and/or freeze. Otherwise, serving madeleines warm from the oven is best!

---

MADELEINE MUST-HAVE:

◇◇◇◇◇◇◇ **MIXER** ◇◇◇◇◇◇◇

To get a fine-grained texture, use either a stand mixer or handheld mixer, which will create more air bubbles in the batter than whisking by hand. The aeration will result in a madeleine that resembles a pound cake when baked.

---

# ❧ TAHITIAN VANILLA BEAN MADELEINES ❧

**THERE IS NOTHING LIKE PURE VANILLA TO ADD SOME "OOMPH" TO BAKED GOODS. BUT** because using vanilla bean pods can be expensive and time-consuming, I use vanilla bean paste. It packs a powerful flavor punch and can be substituted teaspoon for teaspoon for vanilla.

### YIELD: **24** MADELEINES

12 tbsp (1½ sticks) unsalted
  butter, plus 4 tbsp for pans
  (optional)

1 cup granulated sugar

2 large eggs, room temperature

2 tsp vanilla bean paste
  (or vanilla extract)

1 cup all-purpose flour

½ cup confectioners' sugar
  (for finishing)

1. Place a rack in the center of the oven and preheat oven to 350°F. Coat two 12-shell pans with baking spray, or melt an additional 4 tablespoons butter and brush a little in each mold. Set pans aside.

2. Place butter and sugar in a 2-quart microwavable glass bowl or measuring cup. Microwave on low power for 1 to 2 minutes and then stir with a whisk until smooth. If butter is not melted, microwave for 15-second intervals, stirring after each, until mixture is smooth.

3. Let mixture cool for about 3 to 4 minutes and then add eggs, one at a time, whisking well after each addition until completely blended. Then add vanilla and flour and whisk until thoroughly blended.

4. Using a 1½-inch-diameter scoop or a teaspoon, fill shell molds with batter until almost full. Gently press batter to distribute it evenly.

5. Bake for 10 to 12 minutes, until madeleines puff up and gently spring back when pressed lightly.

6. Remove pans from the oven and let cool on a wire rack for 2 to 3 minutes, then invert and tap madeleines onto the rack. You may also use a small offset spatula to remove each one individually. Let cool completely.

7. Once cool, dust the fluted sides with confectioners' sugar.

# ❧ CREAM CHEESE MADELEINES ❧

**CREAM CHEESE ADDS A SUBTLE RICHNESS TO CLASSIC MADELEINES. TO PLAY AROUND** with the flavor even more, substitute orange or lime zest (or a combination of the two) for the lemon zest called for here. I often serve my cream cheese madeleines with fresh raspberries or pots of strawberry preserves as a nod to the fantastic cream cheese and jelly combo.

## YIELD: **24** MADELEINES

12 tbsp (1½ sticks) unsalted butter, room temperature, plus 4 tbsp for pans (optional)

1 cup granulated sugar

4 oz cream cheese (not whipped), cut into small pieces, room temperature

2 large eggs, room temperature

1 tsp freshly grated lemon zest

2 tsp fresh lemon juice

½ tsp vanilla extract

1 cup all-purpose flour

1. Place a rack in the center of the oven and preheat oven to 325°F. Coat two 12-shell pans with baking spray, or melt an additional 4 tablespoons butter and brush a little in each mold.

2. Place butter and sugar in a 2-quart microwavable glass bowl or measuring cup. Microwave on low power for 1 to 2 minutes and then stir mixture with a whisk until smooth (about 3 to 4 minutes). If butter is not melted, continue to microwave for 15-second intervals, stirring after each, until mixture is smooth.

3. Add cream cheese and whisk for another 3 to 4 minutes, until mixture is smooth. A handheld mixer or old-fashioned egg beater helps speed up the mixing.

4. Add eggs, one at a time, whisking well after each addition until completely blended. Then add zest, lemon juice, and vanilla and whisk until thoroughly blended. Stir flour into batter until just incorporated.

5. Using a 1½-inch-diameter scoop or a teaspoon, fill shell molds with batter until almost full. No need to press the batter; it'll spread on its own in the oven.

6. Bake for 11 to 13 minutes, until madeleines puff up and edges are lightly browned.

7. Remove pans from oven and let cool on a wire rack for 2 to 3 minutes, then invert and tap madeleines onto the rack. You may also use a small offset spatula to remove each one individually. Serve warm or let cool completely if storing or freezing.

MADELEINE MUST-HAVE:

## MICROPLANE ZESTER

Chefs and bakers alike will tell you that the Microplane zester is a kitchen necessity. That's because it's so versatile. Whether you want to sprinkle Parmesan cheese over a salad, top a foamy cappuccino with grated dark chocolate, or add flavorful citrus zest to a recipe, all you need is this handheld grater. I love using mine for decorating the plates I use when serving madeleines. A dusting of dark chocolate or orange zest is an easy way to dress up a platter.

# ❧ LEMON POPPY SEED MADELEINES ❧

**THE COMBINATION OF FRESH CITRUSY LEMON AND CRUNCHY POPPY SEEDS TASTES** great in a pound cake, so it's no surprise that this familiar flavor profile is just as appealing in madeleine form. Plus, the smaller size offers a much better chance at portion control!

MADELEINES

### YIELD: <u>24</u> MADELEINES

12 tablespoons (1½ sticks) unsalted butter, room temperature, plus 4 tbsp for pans (optional)

1 cup all-purpose flour

1½ tsp baking powder

1 cup granulated sugar

3 large eggs, room temperature

1 tbsp freshly grated lemon zest, from a medium lemon

1 tbsp fresh lemon juice

1 tsp vanilla extract

1 tbsp poppy seeds

**GLAZE**

1½ cups confectioners' sugar, sifted

2 tbsp fresh lemon juice

1. Place a rack in the center of the oven and preheat oven to 350°F. Coat two 12-shell pans with baking spray, or melt an additional 4 tablespoons butter and brush a little in each mold.

2. In a small bowl, whisk together flour and baking powder.

3. Place butter and sugar in a 2-quart microwavable glass bowl or measuring cup. Microwave on low power for 1 to 2 minutes and then stir mixture with a whisk until smooth. If butter is not melted, microwave for 15-second intervals, stirring after each, until mixture is smooth.

4. Let mixture cool for 3 to 4 minutes and then add eggs, one at a time, whisking well after each addition until completely blended. Add zest, lemon juice, and vanilla and whisk until thoroughly blended.

5. Add flour mixture and poppy seeds to batter and stir until flour is incorporated and batter is smooth.

6. Using a 1½-inch-diameter scoop or a teaspoon, fill shell molds with batter until almost full. Gently press batter to distribute it evenly.

**7.** Bake for 10 to 12 minutes, until madeleines puff up and spring back when lightly pressed.

**8.** Remove pans from oven and let cool on a wire rack for 2 to 3 minutes, then invert and tap madeleines onto the rack. You may also use a small offset spatula to remove each one individually. While the madeleines cool, make the lemon glaze.

## GLAZE

**1.** Stir confectioners' sugar and lemon juice together in a small bowl. While stirring, add water 1 teaspoon at a time until mixture is thin and smooth. Whisk to blend well.

**2.** With a pastry brush, coat each madeleine on the scalloped side with a thin layer of the glaze. Place on a sheet pan and allow glaze to set.

# ❧ MADELEINE CLOUDS ❧

**MELT-IN-YOUR-MOUTH RICH, BUTTERY SHORTBREAD COOKIES ARE KNOWN BY SEVERAL** names: Russian tea cakes, Mexican wedding cookies, Greek *kourambiedes*, or, in the United States, butterballs, which often appear at Christmastime. I have adapted this recipe from that of a dear friend's Greek mother. It calls for hazelnuts, but feel free to substitute walnuts, pecans, almonds, or your favorite nuts. Also, you might want to dust off your stand mixer, which will produce a spongier, more cakelike madeleine. But the one-bowl mixing method works for this recipe too.

## YIELD: **24** MADELEINES

**16 tbsp (2 sticks) unsalted butter, room temperature, plus 4 tbsp for pans (optional)**

**8 tbsp confectioners' sugar, plus an additional 2 to 3 cups for coating and sprinkling**

**2 tsp vanilla bean paste or vanilla extract**

**2¼ cups all-purpose flour**

**¾ cup hazelnuts, toasted and finely chopped**

1. Place a rack in the center of the oven and preheat oven to 350°F. Coat two 12-shell pans with baking spray, or melt an additional 4 tablespoons butter and brush a little in each mold.

2. Place butter and 8 tablespoons of the confectioners' sugar in the bowl of a stand mixer. Beat with the mixer's paddle attachment on medium for about 1 to 2 minutes, then medium high until batter is light and fluffy, about 4 to 5 minutes. Add vanilla and beat for another minute.

3. With mixer on low speed, add flour, scraping down the sides of the bowl with a rubber spatula as necessary. Add nuts, continuing to mix on low speed until incorporated.

4. Using a 1½-inch-diameter scoop or a teaspoon, fill shell molds with batter until almost full. Gently press batter to distribute it evenly.

5. Bake for 10 to 12 minutes, until madeleines puff up and edges are golden brown.

6. Remove pans from oven and let cool on a wire rack for 2 to 3 minutes, then invert and tap madeleines onto the rack. You may also use a small offset spatula to remove each one individually.

7. Sprinkle the remaining 2 to 3 cups confectioners' sugar on a cookie sheet. Immediately place the warm madeleines on top and use your hands to cover them completely in sugar. The sugar should melt into the warm madeleines. Let cool completely.

8. When madeleines are cool, sift the remaining confectioners' sugar over them for a pretty finish.

"If baking is any labor at all, it's a labor of love.
A love that gets passed from generation to generation."
—REGINA BRETT

# ❧ CHAI TEA MADELEINES ❧

MY DAUGHTER, LANEY, HAS FILLED AN ENTIRE SHELF IN OUR PANTRY WITH TEAS: GREEN, black, herbal, white, oolong, chai, and on and on. To reclaim a little shelf space, I decided to brew some and add the reduction to a basic batter. After much experimenting, I discovered that a chai tea latte mix made the best madeleine. These have a rich, mellow flavor and give off a wonderful aroma.

## YIELD: **12** MADELEINES

6 tbsp unsalted butter, room temperature, plus 2 tbsp for pan (optional)

$^1/_2$ cup granulated sugar

1 large egg, room temperature

1 tbsp honey

4 tsp store-bought powdered chai tea latte mix (such as Trader Joe's)

$^1/_2$ cup plus 2 tablespoons all-purpose flour

1. Place a rack in the center of the oven and preheat oven to 325°F. Coat one 12-shell pan with baking spray, or brush with melted butter.

2. Place butter and sugar in a 2-quart microwavable glass bowl or measuring cup. Microwave on low power for 1 to 2 minutes and then stir mixture with a whisk until smooth. If butter is not melted, microwave at 15-second intervals, stirring after each, until mixture is smooth.

3. Let mixture cool for about 3 to 4 minutes, and then add egg and whisk until smooth.

4. Whisk in honey until thoroughly blended. Add the chai tea mix and flour and whisk until batter is smooth.

5. Using a $1^1/_2$-inch-diameter scoop or a teaspoon, fill shell molds with batter until two-thirds full. Gently press batter to distribute it evenly.

6. Bake for 10 to 12 minutes, until madeleines are golden brown around the edges. These don't puff up as much as other madeleines, so watch them carefully to avoid overbaking.

7. Remove pan from oven and let cool on a wire rack for 2 to 3 minutes, then invert and tap madeleines onto the rack. You may also use a small offset spatula to remove each one individually. Serve warm, or let cool completely before storing or freezing.

# ❧ DULCE DE LECHE MADELEINES ❧

**ESPECIALLY COMMON IN DESSERTS OF SOUTH AMERICAN COUNTRIES, DULCE DE LECHE** has grown in popularity in the United States and is now increasingly available in grocery stores (check the international foods aisle). This sweet, thick sauce is made by heating sweetened condensed milk (the term literally translates as "candy of milk"), and its rich, decadent flavor and consistency are similar to caramel. In this recipe I use it in the batter, but you can also serve it on the side or sandwich 1/2 teaspoon between mini madeleines.

## YIELD: **24** MADELEINES OR **72** (OR MORE) MINI MADELEINES

1 cup all-purpose flour

1/2 tsp baking powder

12 tbsp (1 1/2 sticks) unsalted butter, room temperature, plus 4 tbsp for pans (optional)

3/4 cup granulated sugar

1/3 cup canned dulce de leche, room temperature (plus an additional 1/3 cup if making madeleine sandwiches)

2 large eggs, room temperature

1 tsp fleur de sel (optional)

1. Place a rack in the center of the oven and preheat oven to 325°F. Coat two 12-shell pans or four mini madeleine pans with baking spray, or melt an additional 4 tablespoons butter and brush a little in each mold.

2. In a small bowl, whisk together flour and baking powder.

3. Place butter and sugar in a 2-quart microwavable glass bowl or measuring cup. Microwave on low power for 1 to 2 minutes and then stir with a whisk until smooth. If butter is not melted, microwave for 15-second intervals, stirring after each, until mixture is smooth.

4. Whisk in dulce de leche until mixture is smooth.

5. Let mixture cool for about 3 to 4 minutes and then add eggs, one at a time, whisking well after each addition until completely blended. Add flour mixture and blend well. The mixture will be thick.

6. Using a 1 1/2-inch-diameter scoop or a teaspoon, fill shell molds with batter until almost full. Sprinkle a few grains of fleur de sel onto each, if using.

**7.** Bake for 11 to 13 minutes, until madeleines puff up and small cracks appear on the tops. If making mini madeleines, reduce baking time to 3 to 4 minutes.

**8.** Remove pans from oven and let cool on a wire rack for 1 to 2 minutes, then invert and tap madeleines onto the rack.

**9.** To make madeleine sandwiches: Cool the madeleines completely, about 20 minutes, so the filling doesn't melt. Spread about a teaspoon of dulce de leche (half a teaspoon for a mini madeleine) onto the flat side of a madeleine, and then sandwich it with another.

"I think baking cookies is equal to
Queen Victoria running an empire.
There's no difference in how
seriously you take your job, how
seriously you approach your whole life."

—MARTHA STEWART

# ❧ ROSEWATER MADELEINES ❧

**ROSEWATER IS A LIGHT, DELICATE, FRAGRANT ESSENCE MADE BY SOAKING FRESH ROSES** in heated water. It's been used since ancient times for medicinal purposes, in religious ceremonies, as perfumes, and even as a food ingredient. From Indian lassis to English scones, rosewater is still a culinary go-to ingredient. These madeleines are moist on the inside and crisp on the outside, and I like to put a drop or two of red food coloring into the batter to give them a soft pink color. Simpler still, you can sprinkle the batter with pink sugar crystals after scooping into the pans and before baking.

MADELEINES

### YIELD: **24** MADELEINES

12 tbsp (1$^1$/$_2$ sticks) unsalted butter, room temperature, plus 4 tbsp for pans (optional)

1 cup granulated sugar

2 large eggs, room temperature

2 tsp rosewater

$^1$/$_2$ tsp vanilla extract

1 or 2 drops red food coloring and/or $^1$/$_3$ cup pink sugar crystals (optional)

1 cup all-purpose flour

1. Place a rack in the center of the oven and preheat oven to 350°F. Coat two 12-shell pans with baking spray, or melt an additional 4 tablespoons butter and brush a little in each mold.

2. Place butter and sugar in a 2-quart microwavable glass bowl or measuring cup. Microwave on low power for 1 to 2 minutes and then stir mixture with a whisk until smooth. If butter is not melted, microwave for 15-second intervals, stirring after each, until mixture is smooth.

3. Let mixture cool for about 3 to 4 minutes and then add eggs, one at a time, whisking well after each addition until completely blended. Add rosewater and vanilla and whisk until thoroughly blended. If using food coloring, whisk a drop or two into mixture.

4. Add flour and whisk in gently until just incorporated.

5. Using a 1$^1$/$_2$-inch-diameter scoop or a teaspoon, fill shell molds with batter until almost full. If using pink sugar crystals, sprinkle a few onto each.

6. Bake for 11 to 13 minutes, until madeleines puff up and spring back when lightly pressed.

7. Remove pans from oven and let cool on a wire rack for 2 to 3 minutes, then invert and tap madeleines onto rack. You may also use a small offset spatula to remove each one individually.

"Cookies are made of butter and love."

—NORWEGIAN PROVERB

# ❧ PIÑA COLADA MADELEINES ❧

**THE PIÑA COLADA IS PUERTO RICO'S OFFICIAL COCKTAIL, AND THE COMBINATION OF** pineapple, rum, lime, and coconut flavors instantly conjures tropical beaches. These madeleines do the same. For extra crunch and tropical flavor, sprinkle toasted macadamia nuts onto each before baking.

## YIELD: **24** MADELEINES

- ³/₄ cup all-purpose flour
- ³/₄ tsp baking powder
- ¹/₈ tsp salt
- 8 tbsp (1 stick) unsalted butter, room temperature, plus 4 tbsp for pans (optional)
- ³/₄ cup light brown sugar, packed
- ¹/₃ cup canned crushed pineapple with juice
- 1 large egg, room temperature
- 1 tbsp dark rum
- 1¹/₂ cups sweetened coconut, toasted, divided
- ¹/₂ cup white chocolate chips
- ³/₄ cup macadamia nuts (optional)

1. Place a rack in the center of the oven and preheat to 350°F. Coat two 12-shell pans with baking spray, or melt 4 tablespoons butter and brush into each mold.

2. In a small bowl, whisk together flour, baking powder, and salt.

3. Place butter and brown sugar in a 2-quart microwavable glass bowl or measuring cup. Microwave on low power for 1 to 2 minutes and stir with a whisk until smooth. If butter is not melted, microwave for 15-second intervals, stirring after each, until smooth. Cool to room temperature.

4. Whisk in pineapple. Add egg, rum, and 1 cup of the coconut, whisking well to combine.

5. Add flour mixture to the batter, blending well to incorporate. Stir in the white chocolate chips.

6. Using a 1¹/₂-inch-diameter scoop or a teaspoon, fill shell molds with batter until almost full. Gently press batter to distribute it evenly. Sprinkle each one with the remaining ¹/₂ cup coconut and the macadamia nuts, if using.

7. Bake for 10 to 12 minutes, until madeleines puff up and edges are golden brown.

8. Remove pans from oven and let cool for 1 to 2 minutes, then invert and tap madeleines onto a rack. Or use a small offset spatula to remove each one individually.

# ❧ EGGNOG MADELEINES ❧

**EGGNOG IS A CREAMY, VANILLA-Y DRINK ASSOCIATED WITH CHRISTMAS THAT'S OFTEN** spiked with bourbon and garnished with freshly ground nutmeg. These eggnog-infused madeleines are a perfect dessert any time of year, but they're a favorite in my house around the holidays, imparting a festive flavor with or without spirits.

## YIELD: 16 MADELEINES

¾ cup all-purpose flour

½ tsp baking powder

⅛ tsp salt

1 to 1½ tsp freshly grated nutmeg (or 2 tsp ground nutmeg), or to taste, plus more for sprinkling

6 tbsp (¾ stick) unsalted butter, room temperature, plus 4 tbsp for pans (optional)

½ cup granulated sugar

⅓ cup eggnog (Optional: Reduce the eggnog by 1 tbsp and add 1 tbsp bourbon or rum.)

2 eggs

1 tsp vanilla bean paste or vanilla extract

1. Place a rack in the center of the oven and preheat oven to 350°F. Coat two 12-shell pans with baking spray, or melt an additional 4 tablespoons butter and brush a little in each mold.

2. In a small bowl, whisk together flour, baking powder, salt, and nutmeg.

3. Place butter and sugar in a 2-quart microwavable glass bowl or measuring cup. Microwave on low power for 1 to 2 minutes and then stir mixture with a whisk until smooth. If butter is not melted, microwave for 15-second intervals, stirring after each, until mixture is smooth.

4. Let mixture cool for about 3 to 4 minutes and then add eggs, one at a time, whisking well after each addition until completely blended. Stir in vanilla bean paste and blend well. Stir in the eggnog and blend well. Add flour mixture, whisking well to blend completely.

5. Using a 1½-inch-diameter scoop or a teaspoon, fill shell molds with batter until almost full. Grate a small amount of nutmeg over each.

6. Bake for 10 to 12 minutes, until madeleines puff up and edges are golden brown.

7. Remove pans from oven and let cool on a wire rack for 1 to 2 minutes, then invert and tap madeleines onto the rack. You may also use a small offset spatula to remove each one individually.

MADELEINE MUST-HAVE:
## ◇◇◇◇◇◇ FRESHLY GRATED NUTMEG ◇◇◇◇◇◇

You *can* use ground nutmeg, but if you want this mild, sweet, and slightly bitter spice to really pop, buy whole nutmeg and grate it as needed with a fine zester or grater. There's no exact formula for substituting fresh nutmeg for ground, but keep in mind that a little goes much further when you grate the spice yourself.

NOT JUST PLAIN VANILLA

# MORNING MADELEINES

**ALTHOUGH HAVING A SLICE OF LEFTOVER CAKE** or, say, a Dark Chocolate Espresso Madeleine (page 78) with your morning coffee never hurt anyone, these breakfast-themed madeleines may inspire a little less diet guilt. The next time everyone's headed to your house for brunch, serve madeleines made with cream cheese and lox instead of bagels. Or make madeleines that taste just like a blueberry muffin (page 73) or cheese Danish (page 70). It's easy to mix the batter the night before, so your madeleines are ready to pop in the oven first thing in the morning. Waking up to the scent of freshly baked Madeleines au Chocolat (page 54)? Yes, please!

*Banana Pecan Madeleines (page 62) and Blueberry-Cream Madeleines (page 73)*

# ❧ MADELEINES AU CHOCOLAT ❧

**THESE ARE THE MADELEINE VERSION OF** *PAIN AU CHOCOLAT*—**A CLASSIC PUFF PASTRY** filled with chunks of dark chocolate. Even if you don't have the time or patience to make a chocolate-filled croissant at home, these madeleines are a cinch to create and every bit as tasty as what you'd get in a French bakery. The rich taste of the chocolate is a delicious contrast to the vanilla-y cakelet. Serve these warm, when the chocolate in the middle is still gooey.

MADELEINES

## YIELD: 18 TO 20 MADELEINES

- ³/₄ cup all-purpose flour
- ³/₄ tsp baking powder
- 6 tbsp (³/₄ stick) unsalted butter, plus 4 tbsp for pans (optional)
- ²/₃ cup granulated sugar, plus an additional 2 tbsp for sprinkling (optional)
- 2 large eggs, room temperature
- 1 tsp vanilla bean paste or vanilla extract
- 1 tsp freshly grated orange zest
- ¹/₂ cup semisweet or dark chocolate chunks or chips

1. Place a rack in the center of the oven and preheat oven to 350°F. Coat two 12-shell pans with baking spray, or melt an additional 4 tablespoons butter and brush a little in each mold. Set pans aside.

2. In a small bowl, whisk together flour and baking powder.

3. Place butter and sugar in a 2-quart microwavable glass bowl or measuring cup and microwave on low power for 1¹/₂ minutes, or until melted.

4. Let mixture cool for about 3 to 4 minutes and then add eggs, one at a time, whisking well after each addition until completely blended.

5. Add vanilla and orange zest and continue beating for another minute or so, then fold in flour mixture until just blended.

6. Using a 1¹/₂-inch-diameter scoop or a teaspoon, fill shell molds with batter until three-quarters full and then place 3 or 4 chocolate chunks in the center of each mold. Using the tip of a spoon or offset spatula, bury the chocolate in the batter. For a sweeter madeleine, sprinkle lightly with sugar before baking.

7. Bake for 10 to 12 minutes, until madeleines puff up and are golden brown.

8. Remove pans from oven and let cool on a wire rack for 2 to 3 minutes, then use a small offset spatula to remove each one individually. Serve warm.

"Why, sometimes I've believed as many as six impossible things before breakfast."

—LEWIS CARROLL

# LOX, CREAM CHEESE, AND RED ONION MADELEINES

**SUNDAY BRUNCH IN MY HOUSE ALWAYS INVOLVES PLATES OF SMOKED SALMON, CAPERS,** tomatoes, thinly sliced red onion, and bagels with cream cheese—and these madeleines taste amazingly similar. For the most vibrant flavor, use smoked wild salmon and serve these warm.

## YIELD: 14 MADELEINES

¾ cup all-purpose flour

½ tsp baking powder

6 tbsp (¾ stick) salted butter, room temperature, plus 4 tbsp for pans (optional)

2 tbsp granulated sugar

2 large eggs, room temperature

2 oz cream cheese (not whipped), cut into small pieces, room temperature

⅓ cup diced lox

¼ cup diced red onion

1 to 2 tbsp diced fresh scallions

1. Place a rack in the center of the oven and preheat oven to 350°F. Coat two 12-shell pans with baking spray, or melt an additional 4 tablespoons butter and brush a little in each mold.

2. In a small bowl, whisk together flour and baking powder.

3. Place butter and sugar in a 2-quart microwavable glass bowl or measuring cup and microwave on low power for 1½ minutes, or until melted.

4. Let mixture cool for 3 to 4 minutes and then add eggs, whisking well after each, until completely blended.

5. Whisk in cream cheese, or blend with a handheld mixer. If you whisk by hand, the batter will be slightly lumpy.

6. Stir in lox, onions, and scallions until evenly distributed.

7. Using a scoop or a teaspoon, fill shell molds with batter until almost full. Gently press to distribute it evenly.

8. Bake for 10 to 12 minutes, until madeleines puff up and are golden brown.

9. Remove pans from oven and let cool on a wire rack for 2 to 3 minutes, then invert and tap madeleines onto the rack. You may also use a small offset spatula to remove each one individually. Let cool completely before serving.

# ❧ PUMPKIN SPICE MADELEINES ❧

**AUTUMN MEANS FINDING THE PERFECT PUMPKIN FOR CARVING, FINALLY BEING ABLE** to order pumpkin spice lattes again, and baking these pumpkin spice madeleines, which taste just like a slice of the moistest pumpkin bread you've ever eaten. In fact, they're so good, you'll serve them year-round.

## YIELD: **16** MADELEINES
*(18 or 19 madeleines if using walnuts or chocolate chips)*

³/₄ cup all-purpose flour

¹/₂ tsp baking powder

¹/₄ tsp salt

1 tsp ground cinnamon

¹/₂ tsp ground ginger

¹/₂ tsp ground nutmeg

6 tbsp (³/₄ stick) unsalted butter, room temperature, plus 4 tbsp for pans (optional)

¹/₂ cup brown sugar, either light or dark brown, packed

2 large eggs, room temperature

¹/₂ cup canned pumpkin puree (not pumpkin pie filling)

1. Place a rack in the center of the oven and preheat oven to 350°F. Coat two 12-shell pans with baking spray, or melt 4 tablespoons of butter and brush into each mold.

2. In a small bowl, whisk together flour, baking powder, salt, and spices. (Note that you can substitute 2 teaspoons pumpkin pie spice for the cinnamon, ginger, and nutmeg.)

3. Place butter and brown sugar in a 2-quart microwavable glass bowl or measuring cup. Microwave on low power for 1 to 2 minutes and then stir mixture with a whisk until smooth. If butter is not melted, microwave for 15-second intervals, stirring after each, until smooth.

4. Let mixture cool for about 3 to 4 minutes and then add eggs, one at a time, whisking well after each addition until completely blended. Whisk in pumpkin until thoroughly blended.

5. Stir in flour mixture until incorporated. The batter should be smooth. Add walnuts or chocolate chips, if using (this will yield 2 or 3 more madeleines).

**¹/₃ cup toasted walnuts, chopped, or ¹/₃ cup mini chocolate chips (optional)**

6. Using a 1¹/₂-inch-diameter scoop or a teaspoon, fill shell molds with batter until almost full. Gently press batter to distribute it evenly.

7. Bake for 10 to 12 minutes, until madeleines puff up and spring back when lightly pressed.

8. Remove pan from oven and let cool on a wire rack for 2 to 3 minutes, then invert and tap madeleines onto the rack. You may also use a small offset spatula to remove each one individually.

# ❧ MAPLEY GRANOLA MADELEINES ❧

**WHEN I LIVED IN VERMONT, I LOVED THE ANNUAL RITE OF PASSAGE OF TAPPING MAPLE** trees to make syrup. A few years ago my husband, Matt, even tried it out himself. Matt's maple syrup was proof that there's no substitute for the real deal. To make these madeleines I paired maple syrup with granola, two breakfast staples. I love serving them with a small dish of vanilla or plain Greek yogurt.

## YIELD: **12 TO 14** MADELEINES

¾ cup all-purpose flour

¾ tsp baking powder

¼ tsp salt

6 tbsp (¾ stick) unsalted butter, plus 2 tbsp for pans (optional)

¼ cup granulated sugar

¼ cup brown sugar, either light or dark, packed

1 large egg, room temperature

¼ cup real maple syrup (the darker the syrup, the stronger the maple flavor)

1 cup of your favorite granola, either homemade or store bought

1. Place a rack in the center of the oven and preheat oven to 350°F. Coat two 12-shell pans with baking spray, or melt an additional 2 tablespoons butter and brush a little in each mold.

2. In a small bowl, whisk together flour, baking powder, and salt.

3. Place butter and sugars in a 2-quart microwavable glass bowl or measuring cup. Microwave on low for 1 to 2 minutes and then stir mixture with a whisk until smooth. If butter is not melted, microwave for 15-second intervals, stirring after each, until smooth.

4. Let mixture cool for 3 to 4 minutes and then add egg, whisking well until completely blended. Add maple syrup and flour mixture and whisk until thoroughly blended.

5. Using a scoop or a teaspoon, fill shell molds with batter until almost full. Top each with a generous spoonful of granola, gently pressing it into the batter.

6. Bake for 10 to 12 minutes, until madeleines are slightly mounded.

7. Remove pan from oven and let cool on a wire rack for 2 to 3 minutes, then invert and tap madeleines onto the rack. You may also use a small offset spatula to remove each one individually.

# ❧ BANANA PECAN MADELEINES ❧

**WHEN YOU'VE GOT A BUNCH OF OVERRIPE BANANAS IN YOUR FRUIT BASKET THAT YOU** don't want to waste, make these madeleines. They taste just like a slice of moist, rich banana bread.

## YIELD: **12** MADELEINES

- ¹/₂ cup plus 2 tablespoons all-purpose flour
- ¹/₂ tsp baking powder
- ¹/₄ tsp salt
- 6 tbsp (³/₄ stick) unsalted butter, room temperature, plus 2 tbsp for pan (optional)
- ¹/₂ cup dark brown sugar, packed
- 1 large egg, room temperature
- ¹/₂ tsp vanilla bean paste or vanilla extract
- ¹/₃ cup mashed ripe banana (about 1 medium banana)
- ¹/₃ cup toasted unsalted pecans, chopped

1. Place a rack in the center of the oven and preheat oven to 350°F. Coat one 12-shell pan with baking spray, or melt an additional 2 tablespoons butter and brush a little in each mold.

2. In a small bowl, whisk together flour, baking powder, and salt.

3. Place butter and brown sugar in a 2-quart microwavable glass bowl or measuring cup. Microwave on low power for 1 to 2 minutes and then stir mixture with a whisk until smooth. If butter is not melted, microwave for 15-second intervals, stirring after each, until smooth.

4. Let mixture cool for about 3 to 4 minutes and then add egg, whisking well until completely blended. Whisk in vanilla and banana, then add flour mixture and whisk until thoroughly blended. Stir in pecans.

5. Using a 1¹/₂-inch-diameter scoop or a teaspoon, fill shell molds with batter until almost full. Gently press batter to distribute it evenly.

6. Bake for 10 to 12 minutes, until madeleines puff up and edges are golden brown.

7. Remove pan from oven and let cool on a wire rack for 2 to 3 minutes, then invert and tap madeleines onto the rack. You may also use a small offset spatula to remove each one individually.

# ❧ FRANCIE'S APPLE MADELEINES ❧

**APPLE PIE, APPLE TURNOVERS, APPLE UPSIDE DOWN CAKE ... THE FRUIT WE'RE SUPPOSED** to eat every day to keep the doctor away certainly makes a mean pastry. These madeleines are adapted from a recipe my friend Francie shared with me. Her French *grand-maman*, Alice Charbonneau, made an amazing apple turnover, which I transformed into a madeleine (naturally!). Serve them warm with a scoop of vanilla ice cream or, if you're opposed to eating ice cream for breakfast, a dollop of vanilla Greek yogurt.

### YIELD: **24** MADELEINES

10 tbsp (1¼ sticks) unsalted butter, melted and cooled, plus 4 tbsp for pans (optional)

1 cup all-purpose flour

¼ tsp salt

3½ tsp ground cinnamon, divided

2 large eggs, room temperature

⅔ cup granulated sugar, plus more for sprinkling (optional)

2 tsp vanilla extract

1 tsp freshly grated lemon zest

1 cup peeled and chopped apple (small to medium size)

1. Place a rack in the center of the oven and preheat oven to 350°F. Coat two 12-shell pans with baking spray, or melt an additional 4 tablespoons butter and brush a little in each mold.

2. In a small bowl, whisk together flour, salt, and 1½ teaspoons of the cinnamon.

3. Place eggs and sugar in the bowl of a stand mixer fitted with the paddle attachment. Beat on medium speed for 3 to 4 minutes, then increase speed to high and continue to beat until batter is light and fluffy, about 4 to 5 minutes. Add vanilla, the remaining 2 teaspoons cinnamon, and zest and continue beating for another minute.

4. Turn off mixer. Remove bowl from mixer and, using a small rubber spatula, stir in flour mixture until incorporated. Drizzle melted butter over batter and fold in. Add apples and fold into batter.

5. Using a 1½-inch-diameter scoop or a teaspoon, fill shell molds with batter until almost full. Gently press batter to distribute it evenly. If desired, sprinkle a little sugar over each madeleine.

6. Bake for 9 to 12 minutes, until madeleines puff up and edges are golden brown.

7. Remove pans from oven and let cool on a wire rack for 2 to 3 minutes, then invert and tap madeleines onto the rack. You may also use a small offset spatula to remove each one individually.

"Even if I knew that tomorrow the world would go to pieces, I would still plant my apple tree."

—MARTIN LUTHER

# ❧ PEANUT BUTTER AND JELLY MADELEINES ❧

**IT'S THE QUINTESSENTIAL CHILDHOOD SANDWICH FOR GOOD REASON: THE SALTY AND** sweet flavors in a PB&J are an irresistible combination. That's why I had to figure out a way to turn this brown-bag lunch favorite into a madeleine. You can easily personalize these with your favorite jam or swap chunky peanut butter for smooth. Just make sure you serve these madeleines with a glass of ice-cold milk!

## YIELD: **12** MADELEINES

- $^1/_2$ cup all-purpose flour
- $^1/_2$ tsp baking powder
- $^1/_4$ tsp salt (omit if using salted peanut butter)
- 6 tbsp ($^3/_4$ stick) unsalted butter, room temperature, plus 2 tbsp for pan (optional)
- $^1/_2$ cup light or dark brown sugar, firmly packed
- 1 large egg, room temperature
- $^1/_2$ tsp vanilla extract
- $^1/_3$ cup smooth, unsalted natural peanut butter
- $^1/_3$ cup grape jelly (or your favorite flavor)

1. Place a rack in the center of the oven and preheat oven to 325°F. Coat one 12-shell pan with baking spray, or melt an additional 2 tablespoons butter and brush a little in each mold.

2. In a small bowl, whisk together flour, baking powder, and salt (if using).

3. Place butter and brown sugar in a 2-quart microwavable glass bowl or measuring cup and microwave on low power for $1^1/_2$ minutes, or until melted.

4. Let mixture cool for about 3 to 4 minutes and then add egg and vanilla, whisking well. Whisk in peanut butter until completely blended. The batter will be thick, sticky, and shiny.

5. Using a $1^1/_2$-inch-diameter scoop or a teaspoon, fill shell molds with batter until three-quarters full. Gently press batter to distribute it evenly. Place $^1/_2$ teaspoon jelly in each center and press it into the batter slightly.

6. Bake for 10 to 12 minutes, until madeleines puff up and edges are golden brown.

7. Remove pan from oven and let cool on a wire rack for 2 to 3 minutes, then use a small offset spatula to remove each one individually. Let cool completely.

"I think careful cooking is love, don't you?
The loveliest thing you can cook for someone who's
close to you is about as nice a valentine as you can give."

—JULIA CHILD

# ❧ SUNSHINE MADELEINES ❧

**MY LOVE FOR MORNING GLORY MUFFINS INSPIRED ME TO CREATE THESE MADELEINES.**
They taste a little like carrot cake with a hint of pineapple, and the recipe can easily be tweaked
to include the flavors you like best. Feel free to substitute pecans for the walnuts, add raisins and
coconut, or even swap in whole-wheat flour for some or all of the white flour. Serve with bowls of
fluffy whipped cream-cheese spread for a healthy-ish breakfast that tastes more like dessert.

## YIELD: 16 TO 18 MADELEINES

¾ cup all-purpose flour

¾ tsp baking powder

¼ tsp baking soda

⅛ tsp salt

1 tsp ground cinnamon

½ cup light or dark brown
sugar, firmly packed

⅓ cup vegetable oil

1 large egg, room temperature

½ cup crushed pineapple,
drained

½ cup grated carrot (grate in a
food processor to save time)

⅓ cup walnuts or pecans,
chopped

1. Place a rack in the center of the oven and preheat oven to 350°F. Coat two 12-shell pans with baking spray, or melt an additional 4 tablespoons butter and brush a little in each mold.

2. In a small bowl, whisk together flour, baking powder, baking soda, salt, and cinnamon.

3. Place brown sugar and oil in a 2-quart glass bowl or measuring cup and whisk until smooth. Add egg and whisk until completely blended.

4. Add pineapple, carrots, and nuts and stir well to combine. Then add flour mixture, blending well.

5. Using a 1½-inch-diameter scoop or a teaspoon, fill shell molds with batter until almost full. Gently press batter to distribute it evenly.

6. Bake for 10 to 12 minutes, until madeleines puff up and spring back when pressed lightly.

## WHIPPED CREAM-CHEESE SPREAD

½ cup (1 stick) unsalted butter, room temperature

6 oz cream cheese (not whipped)

2 tsp vanilla bean paste or vanilla extract

2¼ cups confectioners' sugar

**7.** Remove pans from oven and let cool on a wire rack for 2 to 3 minutes, then invert and tap madeleines onto the rack. You may also use a small offset spatula to remove each one individually.

## WHIPPED CREAM-CHEESE SPREAD

Place all ingredients in the bowl of a stand mixer fitted with the paddle attachment (or in a medium mixing bowl if using a hand mixer). Beat on low speed for 1 minute, then increase speed to medium-high and continue beating for another 4 to 5 minutes, until mixture is light and fluffy. Spread onto madelines with an offset spatula. Store unused spread in the refrigerator for up to 3 days.

# ⚘ CHEESE DANISH MADELEINES ⚘

**THE ROUND, OFTEN CHEESE-FILLED PASTRIES KNOWN IN THE UNITED STATES AS** Danishes are originally from Vienna, Austria. The combination of flaky, buttery pastry stuffed with a range of fillings–from chocolate and cheese to custard and jam–make them a much-loved morning treat. The ricotta cheese filling in these madeleines tastes rich but light, making them less dense but every bit as tasty as a true danish.

## YIELD: 16 MADELEINES

- 6 tbsp (¾ stick) unsalted butter, room temperature, plus 4 tbsp for pans (optional)
- ½ cup granulated sugar
- 1 large egg plus 1 large egg white
- ½ tsp vanilla extract or vanilla bean paste
- ¼ tsp almond extract
- ½ cup all-purpose flour
- ½ tsp baking powder
- ⅓ cup sliced almonds

1. Place a rack in the center of the oven and preheat oven to 350°F. Coat two 12-shell pans with baking spray, or melt an additional 4 tablespoons butter and brush a little in each mold.

2. Place butter and sugar in a 2-quart microwavable glass bowl or measuring cup. Microwave on low power for 1 to 2 minutes and then stir mixture with a whisk until smooth. If butter is not melted, microwave for 15-second intervals, stirring after each, until smooth.

3. Let mixture cool for about 3 to 4 minutes and then add egg, egg white, and extracts, whisking well until completely blended.

4. In a separate bowl, whisk together flour and baking powder. Stir into butter mixture until completely blended.

5. Using a 1½-inch-diameter scoop or a teaspoon, fill shell molds with batter until almost full. Gently press batter to distribute it evenly. Set pans aside while you make the filling.

## RICOTTA FILLING

$^3/_4$ cup whole-milk ricotta cheese

$^1/_3$ cup granulated sugar

1 large egg yolk

$^1/_2$ tsp freshly grated lemon zest

$^1/_2$ tsp freshly grated orange peel

$^1/_2$ tsp vanilla extract

6. In a medium bowl, place all the ricotta filling ingredients and whisk until thoroughly blended.

7. Place about $^3/_4$ teaspoon of filling into the center of each madeleine; the filling should sink into the batter. Sprinkle sliced almonds over madeleines.

8. Bake for 10 to 12 minutes, until madeleines puff up and edges are golden brown.

9. Remove pans from oven and let cool on a wire rack for 2 to 3 minutes. Use a small offset spatula to remove madeleines one at a time.

# ❧ BLUEBERRY-CREAM MADELEINES ❧

**MY MEMORIES OF CHILDHOOD SUMMERS INCLUDE BIG BOWLS OF PLUMP FRESH BLUE-**berries that my mother put in *everything*: pancakes, blintzes, ice cream sauce, and, of course, muffins. These madeleines are my take on her muffin recipe, and I love serving them right out of the oven with a side of whipped cream cheese (page 69).

## YIELD: **18** MADELEINES

$^1/_2$ cup all-purpose flour

$^1/_2$ tsp baking powder

$^1/_4$ tsp salt

6 tbsp ($^3/_4$ stick) unsalted butter, room temperature

$^3/_4$ cup granulated sugar, divided

2 large eggs, room temperature

1 tsp vanilla bean paste or vanilla extract

1 tbsp heavy or whipping cream

$^3/_4$ cup fresh blueberries (If you substitute frozen blueberries, keep them in the freezer until just before using. Otherwise they will streak the batter blue.)

1. Place a rack in the center of the oven and preheat oven to 350° F. Coat two 12-shell pans with baking spray, or melt an additional 4 tablespoons butter and brush a little in each mold.

2. In a bowl, whisk together flour, baking powder, and salt.

3. Place butter and $^1/_2$ cup of the sugar in a 2-quart micro-wavable glass bowl or measuring cup and microwave on low power for $1^1/_2$ minutes, or until melted.

4. Let mixture cool for about 3 to 4 minutes and then add eggs, one at a time, whisking well after each addition until completely blended.

5. Add vanilla and cream, whisking until completely blended. With a small rubber spatula, gently fold in flour mixture. Stir in blueberries.

6. Using a $1^1/_2$-inch-diameter scoop or a teaspoon, fill shell molds with batter until almost full. Sprinkle madeleines lightly with the remaining $^1/_4$ cup sugar.

7. Bake for 10 to 12 minutes, until madeleines puff up and spring back when pressed gently.

8. Remove pans from oven and let cool on a wire rack for 2 to 3 minutes, then use a small offset spatula to remove madeleines one at a time. Serve warm.

# ❧ ORANGEY CRANBERRY MADELEINES ❧

**THICK SLICES OF ORANGE-CRANBERRY POUND CAKE HAVE ALWAYS BEEN ONE OF MY** customers' favorites. These petite versions have the same wonderful orange and cranberry tang, plus they're studded with toasted walnuts and freshly grated orange rind. Feel free to substitute frozen or bottled orange juice for fresh oranges, or pecans for the walnuts.

## YIELD: 16 MADELEINES

¾ cup all-purpose flour

1 tsp baking powder

¼ tsp baking soda

Pinch salt

6 tbsp (¾ stick) unsalted butter, plus 4 tbsp for pans (optional)

½ cup granulated sugar

1 large egg, room temperature

3 tbsp orange juice

1 tsp freshly grated orange rind

½ tsp vanilla extract

¾ cup fresh or frozen cranberries

½ cup chopped walnuts, toasted

1. Place a rack in the center of the oven and preheat oven to 350°F. Coat two 12-shell pans with baking spray, or melt an additional 4 tablespoons butter and brush a little in each mold.

2. In a small bowl, whisk together flour, baking powder, baking soda, and salt.

3. Place butter and sugar in another bowl and microwave on low power for 1 to 2 minutes, or until melted. Whisk to blend well and then let cool to room temperature.

4. Add egg, whisking well, and then orange juice, rind, and vanilla extract. Blend well.

5. Stir in flour mixture until it just disappears into batter, and then stir in cranberries and walnuts until evenly distributed.

6. Using a 1½-inch-diameter scoop or a teaspoon, fill shell molds with batter until almost full. Gently press batter to distribute it evenly.

7. Bake for 10 to 13 minutes, until madeleines puff up, are golden brown around the edges, and spring back when pressed in the center.

**8.** Remove pans from oven and let cool on a wire rack for 2 to 3 minutes, then invert and tap madeleines onto the rack. You may also use a small offset spatula to remove each one individually.

MADELEINE MUST-HAVE:

## REAMER

Reamers are small handheld kitchen tools used to extract juice from halved citrus fruits. There are many styles available, but my favorite is an old one made from olive wood from Greece. The plump handle offers a comfortable grip that doesn't slip.

# DARK AND DELUXE CHOCOLATE MADELEINES

SHAMELESSLY RICH AND IRRESISTIBLY DECADENT, chocolate madeleines aren't anything like the classic one Proust dunked in his linden tea. In my opinion, they're even tastier! After all, doesn't chocolate make everything better? From the Dark Chocolate Espresso Madeleines (page 78) inspired by my award-winning cookies, to classic chocolate combos such as Stuffed Bittersweet Chocolate Mint Seashells (page 80) and Chocolate-Dipped Peanut Butter Madeleines (page 88), the recipes in this chapter are sure to thrill the chocoholics in your life.

*Chocolate-Dipped Peanut Butter Madeleines (page 88)*
*and Dark Chocolate Espresso Madeleines (page 78)*

# ❧ DARK CHOCOLATE ESPRESSO MADELEINES ❧

**FROM THE MOMENT I BOUGHT MY FIRST MADELEINE PANS AND STARTED CREATING MY**
own recipes, I tried to pack as much chocolate into the batter as I could. This trait served me well when I entered the Ghirardelli Chocolate Company Great American Chocolate Cookie Contest at the San Francisco Fair in 1980 and won the top prize for my "San Francisco Fudge Foggies," a mix between brownies, fudge, and dense chocolate cake. My recipe went on to win the Grand COCO Award for best overall recipe in *Chocolatier* magazine's first Great Chocolate Challenge, and I've adapted it to create these dark chocolate espresso madeleines. I love serving them warm with a scoop of vanilla ice cream.

MADELEINES

## YIELD: **24** MADELEINES

- 1½ sticks (12 tablespoons) unsalted butter

- 1 cup granulated sugar

- 1 cup semisweet or bittersweet chocolate chips (or 4 ounces chopped semisweet chocolate)

- 1 tbsp instant espresso powder dissolved in ⅓ cup warm water (or ⅓ cup strong black coffee, or 2 tablespoons instant coffee crystals dissolved in ⅓ cup warm water)

- 2 large eggs, room temperature

- 1 cup all-purpose flour

1. Place a rack in the center of the oven and preheat oven to 325°F. Coat two 12-shell pans with baking spray, or melt an additional 4 tablespoons butter and brush a little in each mold.

2. Place butter, sugar, chocolate, and espresso in a 2-quart microwavable glass bowl or measuring cup. Microwave on low power for 1 to 2 minutes and then stir mixture with a whisk until smooth. If butter is not melted, microwave for 15-second intervals, stirring after each, until smooth. (Alternatively, you can combine these ingredients in the top of a double boiler over simmering water and stir with a whisk until smooth. Remove from heat.)

3. Let mixture cool for about 3 to 4 minutes and then add eggs, one at a time, whisking well after each addition until completely blended. Add the flour and cocoa, whisking thoroughly. The mixture should be very dark, thick, and shiny.

½ cup unsweetened cocoa
powder, either Dutch-
processed or natural

**CHOCOLATE GLAZE**

**2 cups semisweet chocolate
chips**

**4.** Using a 1½-inch-diameter scoop or a teaspoon, fill shell molds with batter until almost full. Gently press batter to distribute it evenly.

**5.** Bake for 10 to 13 minutes, until madeleines puff up and no shiny spots remain in the centers. Small cracks may appear, but be careful not to overbake.

**6.** Remove pans from oven and let cool on a wire rack for 2 to 3 minutes, then invert and tap madeleines onto the rack. You may also use a small offset spatula to remove each one individually. Let cool completely.

## CHOCOLATE GLAZE

**1.** Place chocolate in a 2-quart microwavable glass bowl or measuring cup. Microwave on low power for 1 to 2 minutes and then stir with a whisk until smooth. If chocolate is not melted, microwave for 15-second intervals, stirring after each, until smooth.

**2.** Place a piece of waxed paper on a cookie sheet or large wire rack. Hold each madeleine by its narrow end and dip one-third of it in the warm chocolate glaze. Lift the madeleine and scrape the flat side along the side of the bowl to remove excess. Place madeleines on the waxed paper and let glaze set, 30 to 60 minutes.

# STUFFED BITTERSWEET
## ❧ CHOCOLATE MINT SEASHELLS ❧

**MINT AND CHOCOLATE COME TOGETHER PERFECTLY IN THIS RECIPE, WHICH IS MY TAKE ON** the peppermint brownies my mom used to make. I love to make these in a seashell pan.

YIELD: **46** SEASHELL-SHAPED COOKIES (OR **24** MADELEINES)

12 tbsp (1½ sticks) unsalted butter, plus 4 tbsp for pans (optional)

1 cup semisweet or dark chocolate chips

2 oz unsweetened chocolate, chopped

1 cup granulated sugar

1½ tsp peppermint extract

2 large eggs, room temperature

1 cup all-purpose flour

½ cup unsweetened cocoa powder, either Dutch-processed or natural

½ cup semisweet chocolate chips

½ cup white chocolate chips

1. Place a rack in the center of the oven and preheat oven to 350°F. Coat two seashell pans or two 12-shell madeleine pans with baking spray, or brush with melted butter.

2. Place butter, chocolate chips, unsweetened chocolate, sugar, and ⅓ cup water in a 2-quart microwavable glass bowl or measuring cup. Microwave on low power for 1½ minutes and then stir mixture with a whisk until smooth. If butter is not melted, microwave for 15-second intervals, stirring after each, until smooth.

3. Let mixture cool for about 3 to 4 minutes and then whisk in peppermint extract and add eggs, one at a time, whisking well after each until completely blended. Add the flour and cocoa, whisking thoroughly.

4. Using a scoop or a teaspoon, fill shell molds with batter until almost full. Place 2 white and 2 semisweet chocolate chips onto each madeleine and press to bury the chips.

5. Bake for 10 to 12 minutes, until madeleines puff up and no shiny spots remain in the centers. Small cracks may appear, but be careful not to overbake.

6. Remove pans from oven and let cool on a wire rack for 2 to 3 minutes, then invert and tap madeleines onto the rack. You may also use a small offset spatula to remove each one individually.

# ✤ MOLTEN MADELEINES ✤

**MOLTEN CHOCOLATE CAKES WERE ALL THE RAGE IN THE 1980S THANKS TO CHEF** Jean-Georges Vongerichten, who is thought to have created the decadent dessert. Some bakers use complicated methods to achieve the soufflé-like cake, but mimicking the silky interior in a madeleine is simple: before baking, place 6 or 7 chocolate chips into the batter in each mold. The chips fall into the middle and remain soft and perfectly gooey long after the madeleines cool.

## YIELD: **24** MADELEINES

¹/₂ cup all-purpose flour

1¹/₂ cups confectioners' sugar

10 tbsp (1¹/₄ sticks) unsalted butter, room temperature, plus 4 tbsp for pans (optional)

4 oz unsweetened chocolate, chopped

8 oz chopped semisweet chocolate or 2 cups semisweet chocolate chips

3 large eggs, room temperature

1 tsp vanilla extract

1 tsp instant coffee crystals

1. Whisk flour and confectioners' sugar together in a bowl.

2. Place a rack in the center of the oven and preheat oven to 350°F. Coat two 12-shell pans with baking spray, or melt an additional 4 tablespoons butter and brush a little in each mold.

3. Place butter and unsweetened and semisweet chocolate in a 2-quart microwavable glass bowl or measuring cup. Microwave on low power for 1¹/₂ minutes and then stir the mixture with a whisk until smooth. If chocolate is not melted, microwave for 15-second intervals, stirring after each, until smooth.

4. Let mixture cool for about 3 to 4 minutes and then add eggs, one at a time, whisking after each addition until completely blended. Add vanilla and coffee crystals, whisking thoroughly. Add flour mixture and whisk until smooth.

## MOLTEN FILLING

²/₃ cup semisweet chocolate
  chips

**5.** Using a 1¹/₂-inch-diameter scoop or a teaspoon, fill shell molds with batter until almost full. Place 6 or 7 chocolate chips in the center of each madeleine and press batter to distribute it evenly and bury the chips.

**6.** Bake for 7 to 8 minutes, until the centers of the madeleines appear dark and shiny and the edges are firm and well baked.

**7.** Remove pans from the oven. For soft, gooey madeleines, immediately transfer them to a plate using an offset spatula. For firmer madeleines, let cool in the pan for 10 to 15 minutes before removing with offset spatula.

"Anything is good if it's made of chocolate."
—JO BRAND

# ❧ SNOWBALL MADELEINES ❧

**DESPITE THEIR FROSTY NAME, THESE CONFECTIONS DELIVER A TROPICAL TANG. THE** tart flavor and strong aroma of Key limes pairs well with the super-sweet white chocolate and confectioners' sugar. If you can't get your hands on Key limes, bottled juice (such as Nellie and Joe's Key West Lime Juice) is an easy great swap and available in most supermarkets.

## YIELD: **24 MADELEINES**

- 12 tablespoons (1¹/₂ sticks) unsalted butter, room temperature, plus 4 tbsp for pans (optional)
- 1¹/₂ cups confectioners' sugar
- 1 tsp freshly grated Key lime zest
- 2 tsp fresh (or bottled) Key lime juice
- 1 large egg, room temperature
- ¹/₂ teaspoon vanilla extract
- ¹/₂ cup all-purpose flour
- 1 cup cornstarch
- 5 oz chopped white chocolate, such as Ghirardelli or Lindt, or 1 cup white chocolate chips

### SUGAR COATING

- 2 cups confectioners' sugar
- White sparkling decorating sugar (optional)

1. Place a rack in the center of the oven and preheat oven to 350° F. Coat two 12-shell pans with baking spray, or melt an additional 4 tablespoons butter and brush a little in each mold.

2. Using a stand mixer or handheld mixer, cream butter and confectioners' sugar on low speed for about 4 to 5 minutes. Add lime zest, lime juice, egg, and vanilla. Increase mixer speed to medium and beat mixture until light and fluffy, about 2 to 3 minutes.

3. Whisk together flour and cornstarch in a separate bowl. Add mixture to the batter and blend on low speed until dry ingredients are just incorporated. Stir in chocolate.

4. Using a scoop or a teaspoon, fill molds with batter until almost full and lightly press batter to distribute it evenly.

5. Bake for 10 to 12 minutes, until edges are lightly browned and tops are puffy.

6. Remove pans from oven and let cool on a wire rack for 2 to 3 minutes. These are delicate, so use a small offset spatula to remove each one individually. Let cool completely.

7. Place madeleines on a cookie sheet lined with waxed paper and top with confectioners' sugar. Lightly sprinkle decorating sugar on top before serving.

# CHOCOLATE CHUNK
# ⊱ GRAND MARNIER MADELEINES ⊰

**THE COMBINATION OF BITTER CHOCOLATE AND SWEET, CITRUS-INFUSED GRAND MARNIER** in this recipe is magical. Want to skip the liquor? A great nonalcoholic substitute for orange liqueur is frozen orange juice concentrate. Bittersweet and extra-dark chocolate stand up well to the sweet orange flavor, so whether you decide to spike these madeleines or not, the chocolate–orange combination is sure to wow.

## YIELD: **24** MADELEINES

12 tbsp (1¹/₂ sticks) unsalted butter, room temperature, plus 4 tbsp for pans (optional)

1 cup granulated sugar

2 large eggs, room temperature

1 tsp orange extract

¹/₂ tsp vanilla extract

1 tsp freshly grated orange zest

¹/₄ cup Grand Marnier or other orange-flavored liqueur, or orange juice concentrate (either frozen or thawed)

1¹/₂ cups all-purpose flour

7 oz bittersweet or semisweet dark chocolate, chopped into chunks

1. Place a rack in the center of the oven preheat oven to 350°F. Coat two 12-shell pans with baking spray, or melt an additional 4 tablespoons butter and brush a little in each mold.

2. Place butter and sugar in a 2-quart microwavable glass bowl or measuring cup. Microwave on low power for 1 to 2 minutes and then stir with a whisk until smooth. If butter is not melted, microwave for 15-second intervals, stirring after each, until smooth.

3. Let mixture cool for about 3 to 4 minutes and then add eggs, one at a time, whisking well after each addition until completely blended. Add extracts, zest, and liqueur, whisking thoroughly. Stir in flour until just combined.

4. Cover batter with plastic wrap and refrigerate until cold, about 30 minutes. (Chilling prevents the chocolate from melting when added to the batter.) Add chocolate, stirring until blended.

5. Using a 1$^1/_2$-inch-diameter scoop or a teaspoon, fill shell molds with batter until almost full. Gently press batter to distribute it evenly.

6. Bake for 11 to 13 minutes, until madeleines puff up and no shiny spots remain in the centers. Small cracks may appear and the edges should be lightly browned; be careful not to overbake.

7. Remove pans from oven and let cool on a wire rack for 2 to 3 minutes, then invert and tap madeleines onto the rack. You may also use a small offset spatula to remove each one individually.

"All you need is love.
But a little chocolate now and then doesn't hurt."
—CHARLES M. SHULTZ

DARK AND DELUXE CHOCOLATE MADELEINES

# CHOCOLATE-DIPPED
## ❧ PEANUT BUTTER MADELEINES ❧

**THIS MADELEINE IS INSPIRED BY ONE OF EVERYONE'S FAVORITE FLAVOR COMBINATIONS:** chocolate and peanut butter. I think the dark and bittersweet chocolate give these madeleines a flavor to rival even Reese's claim to fame. These are crunchy on the outside, chewy on the inside, and just the right amount of rich. One is never enough.

## YIELD: **24** MADELEINES

- ¹/₂ cup (1 stick) unsalted butter, room temperature, plus 4 tbsp for pans (optional)
- 1 cup granulated sugar
- 2 large eggs, room temperature
- ²/₃ cup unsalted, unsweetened peanut butter, chunky or smooth
- 1 tsp vanilla bean paste or vanilla extract
- 1 cup all-purpose flour
- ¹/₂ tsp salt
- 2 cups dark or semisweet chocolate chips, or 8 ounces coarsely chopped semisweet chocolate

1. Place a rack in the center of the oven and preheat oven to 350°F. Coat two 12-shell pans with baking spray, or melt an additional 4 tablespoons butter and brush a little in each mold.

2. Place butter and sugar in a 2-quart microwavable glass bowl or measuring cup. Microwave on low power for 1 to 2 minutes and then stir mixture with a whisk until smooth. If butter is not melted, microwave for 15-second intervals, stirring after each, until smooth.

3. Let mixture cool for about 3 to 4 minutes and then add eggs, one at a time, whisking well after each addition until completely blended. Whisk in peanut butter until well blended. Add vanilla, flour, and salt, whisking until thoroughly incorporated.

4. Using a 1¹/₂-inch-diameter scoop or a teaspoon, fill shell molds with batter until almost full. Gently press batter to distribute it evenly.

5. Bake for 10 to 12 minutes, until madeleines puff up and no shiny spots remain in the centers. Small cracks may

²/₃ cup honey-roasted or plain
peanuts, chopped fine to
medium

appear and edges should be lightly browned; be careful not
to overbake.

6. Remove pans from oven and let cool on a wire rack for
1 to 2 minutes, then invert and tap madeleines onto the
rack. You may also use a small offset spatula to remove
each one individually. Let cool completely.

7. Make a dipping glaze: Place chocolate in a microwavable glass bowl or measuring cup and microwave on low
power for 1 to 2 minutes; stir mixture with a whisk until
smooth. If chocolate is not melted, microwave for 15-
second intervals, stirring after each, until smooth.

8. Line a cookie sheet with waxed paper. Place peanuts in a
wide shallow bowl.

9. To decorate: Hold madeleine at the narrow end, dip
two-thirds into the melted chocolate, and scrap flat side
against the edge of the bowl to remove excess chocolate.
Gently dip into the nuts to coat. Place on sheet pan and
allow to set before serving.

# ❧ KAHLÚA MADELEINES ❧

**THE SUCCESS OF MY AWARD-WINNING SAN FRANCISCO FUDGE FOGGIES IS DUE PARTLY** to the delicious combination of chocolate and coffee. Each flavor enhances the other. Try it in these moist and fudgy Kahlúa madeleines.

## YIELD: **24** MADELEINES

- ³/₄ cup (1¹/₂ sticks) unsalted butter, room temperature, plus 4 tbsp for pans (optional)
- 1 cup granulated sugar
- 4 oz semisweet chocolate, chopped coarsely, or 1 cup semisweet chocolate chips
- 2 large eggs, room temperature
- 1 tsp vanilla bean paste or vanilla extract
- 6 tbsp Kahlúa, another coffee-flavored liqueur, or strong brewed black coffee
- 2 tsp instant coffee (omit if using brewed coffee)
- 1 cup all-purpose flour
- ¹/₂ cup unsweetened cocoa powder, either Dutch-processed or natural, divided
- ¹/₄ cup confectioners' sugar

1. Place a rack in the center of the oven and preheat oven to 350°F. Coat two 12-shell pans with baking spray, or melt an additional 4 tablespoons butter and brush a little in each mold.

2. Place butter, sugar, and chocolate in a 2-quart microwavable glass bowl or measuring cup. Microwave on low for 1 to 2 minutes and then stir mixture with a whisk until smooth. If ingredients are not melted, microwave for 15-second intervals, stirring after each, until smooth.

3. Let mixture cool for about 3 to 4 minutes and then add eggs, one at a time, whisking well after each addition until completely blended. Add vanilla, whisking thoroughly.

4. In a separate bowl, mix Kahlúa and coffee, add to the chocolate mixture, and whisk well. Add ¼ cup cocoa powder and flour and mix well. The mixture will be dark, thick, and shiny.

5. Using a scoop or a teaspoon, fill molds with batter until almost full. Gently press batter to distribute it evenly.

6. Bake for 11 to 14 minutes, until madeleines puff up and no shiny spots remain in the centers. Small cracks may appear, but be careful not to overbake.

7. Remove pans from oven and let cool on a wire rack for 2 to 3 minutes, then remove each madeleine individually using a small offset spatula. Let cool completely. For a pretty and tasty finish, sift confectioners' sugar and/or cocoa powder over cooled madeleines.

# ❧ ROCKY ROAD MADELEINES ❧

**WE HAVE SAM ALTSHULER, A RUSSIAN IMMIGRANT TO THE UNITED STATES, TO THANK** for the sublime creation called the Rocky Road candy bar, which he sold from a pushcart on Market Street in San Francisco in the early 1950s. The mix of milk chocolate, marshmallows, vanilla, and cashews remains a favorite in the form of Rocky Road candy, fudge, and ice cream. Translating this combination of flavors and textures into a madeleine is a lot of fun, and this version is wide open to personalization. You can substitute milk chocolate chips for the semisweet chips and cashews for walnuts, or use your imagination and toss in another tasty ingredient.

## YIELD: **24** MADELEINES

²/₃ cup all-purpose flour

¹/₂ cup unsweetened cocoa powder, either Dutch-processed or natural

³/₄ cup (1¹/₂ sticks) unsalted butter, room temperature, plus 4 tbsp for pans (optional)

1 cup granulated sugar

2 large eggs, room temperature

1 cup semisweet chocolate chips, or 4 ounces chopped semi-sweet or bittersweet chocolate

1 cup toasted walnuts, coarsely chopped

1 cup miniature marshmallows

1. Place a rack in the center of the oven and preheat oven to 350°F. Coat two 12-shell pans with baking spray, or melt an additional 4 tablespoons butter and brush a little in each mold.

2. In a small bowl, whisk together flour and cocoa powder.

3. Place butter and sugar in a 2-quart microwavable glass bowl or measuring cup. Microwave on low power for 1 to 2 minutes, until melted, and then stir mixture with a whisk until smooth. If butter is not melted, microwave for 15-second intervals, stirring after each, until smooth.

4. Let mixture cool for about 3 to 4 minutes and then add eggs, one at a time, whisking well after each addition until completely blended. Add flour mixture, whisking well, then add chocolate and nuts, stirring until blended. The batter will be dark, shiny, and sticky.

5. Using a 1¹/₂-inch-diameter scoop or a teaspoon, fill shell molds with batter until almost full. Gently press batter to distribute it evenly.

6. Bake for 7 to 9 minutes, until madeleines puff up and no shiny spots remain in the centers. Small cracks may appear and the edges should be lightly browned; be careful not to overbake.

7. Remove pans from oven, leaving the oven turned on. Firmly press 3 to 5 mini marshmallows into each madeleine, but do not bury them. Return pans to oven for 1 to 2 minutes to lightly brown marshmallows.

8. Remove pans from oven and let cool on a wire rack for 2 to 3 minutes, then use a small offset spatula to remove each one individually. Let cool completely.

"Strength is the capacity to break a chocolate bar into four pieces with your bare hands—and then eat just one piece."

–JUDITH VIORST

# ⁂ ESPRESSO CHIP MADELEINES ⁂

WHEN COCOA AND COFFEE BEANS CONVERGE, MOCHA IS BORN—AND AS A MOCHA latte devotee, I felt compelled to create a dark chocolate madeleine with a strong espresso flavor. Increase the espresso powder or add a tablespoon or two of freshly brewed espresso for an even richer coffee flavor. Just be careful not to eat these madeleines too late in the evening (unless you're trying to pull an all-nighter) because they pack a hefty dose of caffeine!

### YIELD: 18 MADELEINES

1¼ cups all-purpose flour

2 tsp baking powder

⅛ tsp salt

2 tbsp instant espresso powder, or more to taste

1 tbsp hot water

5 tbsp unsalted butter, room temperature, plus 4 tbsp for pans (optional)

½ cup sugar

2 large eggs, room temperature

½ cup whole milk

½ cup dark chocolate chunks, chips, or mini chips

1. Place a rack in the center of the oven and preheat oven to 350°F. Coat two 12-shell pans with baking spray, or melt an additional 4 tablespoons butter and brush a little in each mold.

2. Whisk together flour, baking powder, and salt in a small bowl and set aside. In another small bowl, whisk together espresso powder and hot water to make a paste.

3. Place butter and sugar in a 2-quart microwavable glass bowl or measuring cup. Microwave on low power for 1 to 2 minutes and then stir mixture with a whisk until smooth. If butter is not melted, microwave for 15-second intervals, stirring after each, until smooth.

4. Let mixture cool for about 3 to 4 minutes and then add eggs, one at a time, whisking well after each addition until completely blended. Add milk and blend well, then add flour mixture, whisking until completely blended.

5. Add espresso mixture, stirring well, and then fold in chocolate.

6. Using a $1^{1}/_{2}$-inch-diameter scoop or a teaspoon, fill shell molds with batter until almost full. Gently press batter to distribute it evenly.

7. Bake for 10 to 12 minutes, until madeleines puff up and the tops spring back when gently pressed; be careful not to overbake.

8. Remove pans from oven and let cool on a wire rack for 2 to 3 minutes, then use a small offset spatula to remove each one individually. Let cool completely.

"There's no metaphysics on earth like chocolates."
—FERANDO PESSOA

DARK AND DELUXE CHOCOLATE MADELEINES

# ⁃ NUTELLA PARFAIT MADELEINES ⁃

**ALTHOUGH THE WORD** *PARFAIT* **MAY INSPIRE MOST PEOPLE TO THINK OF FRUIT AND** granola, in my world it means layer upon layer of my all-time favorite food: Nutella. The hazelnut liqueur in the batter further deepens the chocolate-hazelnut spread's flavor, and the bittersweet chocolate glaze adds richness.

## YIELD: **24** MADELEINES

1 cup all-purpose flour

¹/₂ cup unsweetened natural cocoa powder

³/₄ cup (1¹/₂ sticks) unsalted butter, room temperature

1 cup sugar

1 cup semisweet chocolate chips or 4 ounces chopped semisweet chocolate

2 large eggs, room temperature

2 tsp Frangelico or other hazelnut liqueur, or vanilla extract

²/₃ cup Nutella or other chocolate-hazelnut spread

1. Place a rack in the center of the oven and preheat oven to 350°F. Coat two 12-shell pans with baking spray, or melt an additional 4 tablespoons butter and brush a little in each mold.

2. In a medium bowl, whisk together flour and cocoa powder.

3. Place butter, sugar, and chocolate in a 2-quart microwavable glass bowl or measuring cup. Microwave on low power for 1 to 2 minutes and then stir mixture with a whisk until smooth. If ingredients are not melted, microwave for 15-second intervals, stirring after each, until smooth. (Alternatively, you can combine these ingredients in the top of a double boiler over simmering water and stir with a whisk until smooth. Remove from heat.)

4. Let mixture cool for about 3 to 4 minutes and then add eggs, one at a time, whisking well after each addition until completely blended. Mix in liqueur or extract. Whisk in flour mixture until smooth. The batter will be sticky, thick, and shiny.

## BITTERSWEET GLAZE

**4 oz chopped unsweetened chocolate**

**2 cups semisweet chocolate chips or 8 ounces coarsely chopped semisweet chocolate**

**5.** Using a $1^{1}/_{2}$-inch-diameter scoop or a teaspoon, fill shell molds with batter until almost full. Gently press batter to distribute it evenly.

**6.** Bake for 11 to 13 minutes, until madeleines puff up and no shiny spots remain in the centers. It's okay if small cracks appear, but be careful not to overbake.

**7.** Remove pans from oven and let cool on a wire rack for 2 to 3 minutes, then invert and tap madeleines onto the rack. You may also use a small offset spatula to remove each one individually. Let cool completely.

**8.** Spread 1 teaspoon Nutella on the flat side of each madeleine, place them on a sheet pan lined with waxed paper, and refrigerate for 30 minutes.

**9.** Make the glaze: Place unsweetened and semisweet chocolate chips in a 2-quart microwavable glass bowl or measuring cup. Microwave on low power for 1 to 2 minutes and then stir with a whisk until smooth. If chocolate is not melted, microwave for 15-second intervals, stirring after each, until smooth.

**10.** Place a piece of waxed paper on a cookie sheet or large wire rack. Dip the flat side of each into the glaze, being sure to cover the Nutella completely. (Alternatively, you may spread a thin coating of glaze over the Nutella layer using an offset spatula.) Place madeleines glazed side up on prepared cookie sheet and let set completely, 30 to 60 minutes.

# FRUIT AND NUTS

**WHEN IT COMES TO ADDING FRUIT OR NUTS (OR** both) to baked goods, the possibilities are endless. Fresh-picked, dried, or frozen fruit and a plethora of nuts can yield countless variations of cakes, cookies, and, of course, madeleines. The recipes in this chapter call for everything from wild blueberries, dried cherries, and shredded coconut to raw almonds, roasted pecans, and toasted walnuts. They're so easy (and tasty!), they may even inspire you to experiment with your own fruit-and-nut combinations.

*White Chocolate, Hazelnut, and Cherry Madeleines (page 108)*

# ❧ JOYFUL MADELEINES ❧

**CHOCOLATE, SWEET COCONUT, AND ALMONDS ARE THE HABIT-FORMING COMBINATION** found in Almond Joy candy bars, which inspired these madeleines. The chocolate glaze covering the almonds imparts an elegant look that's as delicious as it is beautiful.

## YIELD: 12 TO 14 MADELEINES

- $1/2$ cup all-purpose flour
- $1/4$ tsp salt
- 6 tbsp unsalted butter, room temperature, plus 4 tbsp for pans (optional)
- $1/2$ cup granulated sugar
- 1 large egg, room temperature
- $3/4$ tsp almond extract
- $1/3$ to $1/2$ cup sweetened shredded coconut
- 24 whole roasted unsalted almonds

1. Place a rack in the center of the oven and preheat to 350°F. Coat a 12-shell pan with baking spray, or melt 4 tablespoons butter and brush a little in each mold.

2. In a small bowl, whisk together flour and salt.

3. Place butter and sugar in a 2-quart microwavable glass bowl or measuring cup and microwave on low power for $1^1/2$ minutes, or until melted.

4. Let mixture cool for about 3 to 4 minutes and then add egg and almond extract, whisking until completely blended. Add coconut and continue beating for another minute or so; fold in flour mixture until just blended.

6. Using a scoop or a teaspoon, fill shell molds with batter until three-quarters full. Place 2 whole almonds lengthwise in each mold and gently press into batter.

7. Bake for 12 to 14 minutes, until madeleines puff up and are golden brown.

8. Remove pans from the oven and let cool on a wire rack for 2 to 3 minutes, then invert and tap madeleines onto the rack. You may also use a small offset spatula to remove each one individually.

## CHOCOLATE GLAZE

1¹/₃ cups semisweet chocolate
   chips or chopped dark
   chocolate

## TO DECORATE

1. Place chocolate in a 2-quart microwavable glass bowl
   or measuring cup. Microwave on low power for 1 to
   2 minutes and then stir with a whisk until smooth. If
   chocolate is not melted, microwave for 15-second intervals, stirring after each, until smooth.

2. Place a piece of waxed paper on a cookie sheet or large
   wire rack. Dip the flat side (the one with the almonds)
   of each madeleine into the glaze, scraping along the side
   of the bowl to remove excess. Alternatively, you can use
   a small offset spatula to glaze. Place glazed madeleines
   on the prepared cookie sheet and let set for 30 to 60
   minutes (or refrigerate to set more quickly).

# ❧ PEACHES AND CREAM MADELEINES ❧

**NOTHING SAYS SUMMER LIKE A BIG JUICY PEACH—AND THESE MADELEINES ARE EVERY** bit as moist, tender, fragrant, and delicious as what Mother Nature makes herself.

## YIELD: 12 MADELEINES

- ½ cup all-purpose flour
- ¼ tsp baking powder
- ⅛ tsp salt
- 1 tsp ground cinnamon, divided
- 6 tbsp (¾ stick) unsalted butter, plus 2 tbsp for pan (optional)
- ¾ cup granulated sugar, divided
- 3 oz cream cheese, room temperature, cut into small pieces
- 1 large egg, room temperature
- ⅓ cup drained and chopped canned peaches (look for ones packed "in their own juice," not sweetened liquid), or ⅓ cup chopped fresh peaches

1. Place a rack in the center of the oven and preheat oven to 350°F. Coat one 12-shell pan with baking spray, or melt an additional 2 tablespoons butter and brush a little in each mold.

2. In a small bowl, whisk together flour, baking powder, salt, and half the cinnamon.

3. Place butter and ½ cup of the sugar in another bowl and microwave on low power for 1 to 2 minutes, or until melted. Whisk to blend well and then set aside to let cool to room temperature.

4. Add cream cheese, whisking well, and then add egg, continuing to whisk until batter is smooth.

5. Stir in flour mixture just until it disappears into batter, and then stir in peaches.

6. Using a 1½-inch-diameter scoop or a teaspoon, fill shell molds with batter until almost full. Combine the remaining sugar and cinnamon and lightly sprinkle mixture over the madeleines for added flavor and sparkle.

7. Bake for 10 to 13 minutes, until madeleines puff up and edges are golden brown.

8. Remove pans from oven and let cool on a wire rack for 2 to 3 minutes, then use a small offset spatula to remove each one individually.

# ❧KENTUCKY DERBY MADELEINES❧

**THE KENTUCKY DERBY OFFERS FANS "THE MOST EXCITING TWO MINUTES IN SPORTS."** Of course, another draw is the food served at Derby gatherings. From mint juleps to chocolate-bourbon pecan pie, bourbon is a must, and it has inspired these madeleines.

## YIELD: **24 MADELEINES**

1¼ cups all-purpose flour

¼ tsp salt

¾ cup (1½ sticks) unsalted butter, room temperature

1 cup dark or light brown sugar, firmly packed

2 eggs, room temperature

2 tsp bourbon (or substitute vanilla extract)

1 cup pecans, toasted and chopped

¾ cup finely chopped dark chocolate, such as Scharffen-Berger 62% semisweet chocolate

1. Place a rack in the center of the oven and preheat oven to 350°F. Coat two 12-shell pans with baking spray, or melt an additional 4 tablespoons butter and brush a little in each mold.

2. In a small bowl, whisk together flour and salt.

3. Place butter and sugar in a 2-quart microwavable glass bowl or measuring cup. Microwave on low power for 1 to 2 minutes and then stir mixture with a whisk until smooth. If butter is not melted, microwave for 15-second intervals, stirring after each, until smooth.

4. Let mixture cool for about 3 to 4 minutes and then add eggs, one at a time, whisking well after each addition until completely blended.

5. Add bourbon and stir to blend in thoroughly. Stir in flour mixture until completely incorporated; add nuts and chocolate and stir until just mixed in.

6. Using a 1½-inch-diameter scoop or a teaspoon, fill shell molds with batter until three-fourths full. Gently press batter to distribute it evenly. Bake for 11 to 13 minutes, until madeleines puff up and edges are golden brown.

7. Remove pans from oven and let cool on a wire rack for 2 to 3 minutes, then invert and tap madeleines onto rack. You may also use a small offset spatula to remove each one individually.

# ⤝ GRADE B MAPLE SYRUP MADELEINES ⤞

**"GRADE A" SOUNDS LIKE IT WOULD BE THE BEST, BUT FOR MAPLE SYRUP THE DESIGNATION** just means that the color and flavor is more delicate than grade B syrup, which is made from sap collected later in the season. The robust flavor of grade B maple syrup stands up well to the toasted walnuts in this madeleine, though any pure maple syrup will work well.

### YIELD: **12** MADELEINES

½ cup all-purpose flour

¼ tsp salt

½ tsp baking powder

6 tbsp (¾ stick) unsalted butter, room temperature, plus 2 tbsp for pan (optional)

⅓ cup granulated sugar

1 large egg, room temperature

¼ cup grade B maple syrup, or any pure maple syrup

½ cup toasted walnuts chopped somewhat coarsely

1. Place a rack in the center of the oven and preheat oven to 350°F. Coat one 12-shell pan with baking spray, or melt an additional 2 tablespoons butter and brush a little in each mold.

2. In a small bowl, whisk together flour, salt, and baking powder.

3. Place butter and sugar in a 2-quart microwavable glass bowl or measuring cup and microwave on low power for 1½ minutes, or until melted.

4. Let mixture cool for 1 to 2 minutes and then add egg and maple syrup, whisking well until completely blended. Add flour mixture and stir until completely incorporated.

5. Using a 1½-inch-diameter scoop or a teaspoon, fill shell molds until three-quarters full. Sprinkle each madeleine with walnuts.

6. Bake for 10 to 12 minutes, until madeleines mound up slightly and spring back when gently pressed.

7. Remove pans from oven and let cool on a wire rack for 2 to 3 minutes, then invert and tap madeleines onto the rack. You may also use a small offset spatula to remove each one individually.

# ❖FRESH LEMON DROP MADELEINES❖

**PUCKERINGLY TART AND SWEET AT THE SAME TIME, THESE MADELEINES ARE AS TASTY AS** they are messy. Think of them as a lemon-soaked Bundt cake in shell form. My best advice is to serve these tasty tea cakes with large napkins. They'll leave everyone's fingers sticky, but they're so buttery and lemony that nobody will care.

## YIELD: **24** MADELEINES

1¼ cups all-purpose flour

½ tsp baking powder

¾ cup (1½ sticks) unsalted butter, room temperature, plus 4 tbsp for pans (optional)

1½ cups granulated sugar, divided

2 large eggs, room temperature

1 tbsp freshly grated lemon zest (from 1 medium lemon)

½ cup plus 1 tablespoon lemon juice (fresh, bottled, or a combination), divided

¼ tsp lemon extract

½ tsp vanilla extract

1 tbsp cream, half-and-half, or milk

1 to 2 cups confectioners' sugar

1. Place a rack in the center of the oven and preheat oven to 350°F. Coat two 12-shell pans with baking spray, or melt 4 tablespoons butter and brush a little in each mold.

2. In a small bowl, whisk together flour and baking powder.

3. Place butter and 1 cup of the granulated sugar in a 2-quart microwavable glass bowl or measuring cup. Microwave on low power for 1 to 2 minutes, then stir mixture with a whisk until smooth. If butter is not melted, microwave for 15-second intervals, stirring after each, until smooth.

4. Let mixture cool for about 3 to 4 minutes and then add eggs, one at a time, whisking well after each until completely blended. Add zest, 1 tablespoon of the lemon juice, extracts, and cream. Whisk until thoroughly blended, about a minute.

5. Stir in flour mixture until completely incorporated.

6. Using a scoop or a teaspoon, fill shell molds with batter until three-quarters full. Bake for 11 to 13 minutes, until madeleines puff up and edges are golden brown.

7. Remove pans from oven and let cool on a wire rack for 2 to 3 minutes, then invert and tap madeleines onto the rack. You may also use a small offset spatula to remove each one individually.

**8.** Make a soaking syrup by combine the remaining $^1/_2$ cup lemon juice and $^1/_2$ cup granulated sugar in a small saucepan over medium heat. While stirring, bring mixture to a boil. Boil for about a minute, stirring, until sugar dissolves, then lower heat to a simmer and cook for another minute, continuing to stir. Remove from heat.

## TO ASSEMBLE

**1.** With a toothpick, poke several holes in the flat side of each madeleine. Spoon about 1 teaspoon of the lemon syrup over each madeleine, allowing it to soak in. Repeat if you want super-lemony madeleines.

**2.** Turn over madeleines and sprinkle confectioners' sugar all over the rounded sides.

"I'm just someone who likes cooking
and for whom sharing food is a form of expression."
—MAYA ANGELOU

# WHITE CHOCOLATE, HAZELNUT, AND CHERRY MADELEINES

**WANT TO MAKE A BAKED GOOD EVEN BETTER? ADD SOME FRUIT AND NUTS! THIS DUO** has long been a go-to ingredient combination for professional and home bakers alike, probably because salty-sweet concoctions always turn out so delicious. White chocolate, hazelnuts, and sweet dried cherries are no exception to this rule.

## YIELD: 12 MADELEINES

- ½ cup all-purpose flour
- ¼ tsp baking powder
- ¼ tsp salt
- 5 tbsp unsalted butter, room temperature, plus 2 tbsp for pans (optional)
- ½ cup granulated sugar
- 1 large egg, room temperature
- 1 tsp vanilla extract
- ⅓ cup toasted and coarsely chopped hazelnuts
- ⅓ cup white chocolate chips
- ¼ cup sweetened dried organic cherries, chopped

1. Place a rack in the center of the oven and preheat to 350°F. Coat one 12-shell pan with baking spray, or melt 2 tablespoons butter and brush some in each mold.

2. In a small bowl, whisk together flour, baking powder, and salt.

3. Place butter and sugar in a 2-quart microwavable glass bowl or measuring cup and microwave on low power for 1½ minutes, or until melted.

4. Add egg and vanilla, whisking well until blended. Add flour mixture and whisk until completely incorporated. Stir in nuts, white chocolate, and cherries until evenly distributed.

5. Using a scoop or a teaspoon, fill shell molds with batter until three-quarters full. Bake for 11 to 13 minutes, until madeleines puff up and edges are golden brown.

6. Remove pan from oven and let cool on a wire rack for 2 to 3 minutes, then invert and tap madeleines onto the rack. You may also use a small offset spatula to remove each one individually.

# LORRAINE'S CHOCOLATE, DATE,
## ❧ AND WALNUT MADELEINES ❧

MY MOTHER, LORRAINE, WAS A FANTASTIC COOK AND BAKER WHO HAD SO MANY SPE-cialties, we rarely ate the same meal or dessert twice. One exception was her über-moist chocolate, date, and walnut cake, which she'd bake several times a month. These madeleines are inspired by her go-to confection.

## YIELD: 14 MADELEINES

- ¹/₂ cup pitted dates (about 12), chopped
- ¹/₃ cup boiling water
- ³/₄ cup all-purpose flour
- ¹/₄ tsp baking powder
- 2 tbsp unsweetened natural cocoa powder
- 6 tbsp (³/₄ stick) unsalted butter, room temperature, plus 4 tbsp for pans (optional)
- ¹/₂ cup granulated sugar
- 1 large egg, room temperature
- ¹/₂ tsp vanilla extract
- ¹/₃ cup walnuts, toasted and chopped
- ¹/₃ cup (or more!) mini or regular-size semisweet chocolate chips (or chopped semisweet or dark chocolate)

1. Place a rack in the center of the oven and preheat oven to 350°F. Coat two 12-shell pans with baking spray, or melt an additional 4 tablespoons butter and brush a little in each mold.

2. Set dates aside to soak in a bowl of boiling water.

3. In a small bowl, whisk together flour, baking powder, and cocoa powder.

4. Place butter and sugar in a 2-quart microwavable glass bowl or measuring cup and microwave on low power for 1¹/₂ minutes, or until melted.

5. Add egg and vanilla extract, whisking until smooth, then add flour mixture and whisk until just blended in. Add dates and their soaking liquid and stir until evenly distributed.

6. Using a scoop or a teaspoon, fill molds with batter until three-fourths full. Sprinkle the walnuts and chocolate chips on top and gently press them into the batter. Bake for 10 to 12 minutes, until madeleines puff up and spring back when gently pressed.

7. Remove pans from oven and let cool on a wire rack for 2 to 3 minutes, then invert and tap madeleines onto the rack. You may also use a small offset spatula to remove each one individually.

# ❧ ALMOND MACAROON MADELEINES ❧

**ALMOND MACAROONS ARE SOFT, CHEWY COOKIES FLAVORED WITH LEMON, AND THE** ingredients that make them so delicious are just as tasty in a madeleine. The layer of sliced almonds adds crunchy texture to the extra-chewy center.

## YIELD: **24** MADELEINES

<sup></sup>3/4 cup (1<sup></sup>1/2 sticks) unsalted butter, room temperature, plus 4 tbsp for pans (optional)

1 cup granulated sugar

1/3 cup canned almond cake and pastry filling (not almond paste), such as Solo

2 large eggs, room temperature

1/2 tsp lemon extract

1/2 tsp almond extract

1 tsp freshly grated lemon zest

1 cup all-purpose flour

1 cup sliced almonds

1. Place a rack in the center of the oven and preheat oven to 350°F. Coat two 12-shell pans with baking spray, or melt an additional 4 tablespoons butter and brush a little in each mold. Set pans aside.

2. Place butter and sugar in a 2-quart microwavable glass bowl or measuring cup. Microwave on low power for 1 to 2 minutes and then stir mixture with a whisk until smooth. If butter is not melted, microwave for 15-second intervals, stirring after each, until smooth.

3. Add almond filling and whisk until completely incorporated.

4. Add eggs, one at a time, whisking well after each until blended. Add extracts and zest, whisking until thoroughly blended, about a minute. Stir in the flour and blend well.

5. Using a scoop or a teaspoon, fill shell molds with batter until three-quarters full. Sprinkle almonds over each.

6. Bake for 10 to 12 minutes, until madeleines puff up and edges are golden brown.

7. Remove pans from oven and let cool on a wire rack for 2 to 3 minutes, then invert and tap madeleines onto the rack. Or use a small offset spatula to remove them.

# ❧ MENDIANT MADELEINES ❧

**WHAT ARE *MENDIANTS*, YOU WONDER? THEY ARE PERFECT CIRCLES OF CHOCOLATE** with a variety of dried fruits and nuts arranged on top. These traditional French candies are served at Christmastime, and each of the toppings represent the four monastic orders: the Carmelites were represented by almonds, the Dominicans by raisins, the Franciscans by figs, and the Augustinians by hazelnuts. Use these ingredients for traditional mediant madeleines, or decorate them with your favorite dried fruits and nuts.

## YIELD: **24** MADELEINES

- ¾ cup all-purpose flour
- ⅓ cup unsweetened cocoa powder, either Dutch-processed or natural
- ¼ tsp salt
- ¾ cup (1½ sticks) unsalted butter, room temperature, plus 4 tbsp for pans (optional)
- ½ cup granulated sugar
- 2 large eggs, room temperature
- 1¼ tsp vanilla extract
- 4 oz semisweet or bittersweet chocolate cut into coarse chunks

1. Place a rack in the center of the oven and preheat oven to 350°F. Coat two 12-shell pans with baking spray, or melt an additional 4 tablespoons butter and brush a little in each mold.

2. In a small bowl, whisk together flour, cocoa powder, and salt.

3. Place butter and sugar in a 2-quart microwavable glass bowl or measuring cup. Microwave on low power for 1 to 2 minutes, until melted, and then stir mixture with a whisk until smooth. If butter is not melted, microwave for 15-second intervals, stirring after each, until smooth.

3. Let mixture cool for about 3 to 4 minutes and then add eggs, one at a time, whisking well after each addition until completely blended. Whisk in vanilla until thoroughly blended. Stir in flour mixture until completely incorporated. The batter should be smooth.

4. Using a 1½-inch-diameter scoop or a teaspoon, fill shell molds with batter until three-quarters full. If necessary, gently press batter to distribute it evenly. Place a chocolate

¹/₃ cup mixed unsalted nuts such as pecans, walnuts, cashews, almonds, macadamia nuts, or Brazil nuts (chop large nuts into smaller pieces)

¹/₃ cup unsulphured dried fruit, such as sweetened cranberries, apricots, cherries, figs, or raisins (cut larger fruit into smaller pieces)

chunk and a few pieces of nuts and fruit in each center and press lightly into the batter.

5. Bake for 11 to 13 minutes, until madeleines puff up and edges are golden brown.

6. Remove pans from oven and let cool on a wire rack for 2 to 3 minutes, then invert and tap madeleines onto the rack. You may also use a small offset spatula to remove each one individually.

# ❧ BROWNED BUTTER PECAN MADELEINES ❧

**BROWNING THE BUTTER MAY SEEM LIKE AN UNNECESSARY STEP IN THIS RECIPE, BUT** trust me—the smidge of extra time and effort is worth it. The browned butter gives these madeleines an amazing nutty aroma that adds depth of flavor and results in a rich, golden brown color.

## YIELD: 16 MADELEINES

5 tbsp unsalted butter, cut into 5 pieces, plus 4 tbsp for pans (optional)

2 large eggs, room temperature

$^1/_4$ cup dark brown sugar, firmly packed

$^1/_4$ cup granulated sugar

2 tsp vanilla extract

$^1/_2$ cup all-purpose flour

$^1/_3$ to $^1/_2$ cup pecans, toasted and coarsely chopped

1. Place a rack in the center of the oven and preheat oven to 350°F. Coat two 12-shell pans with baking spray, or melt an additional 4 tablespoons butter and brush a little in each mold.

2. Melt butter in a heavy-bottomed saucepan over medium-low heat, whisking frequently, until it foams. Continue whisking as the butter foams; as soon as you see little brown bits on the bottom of the pan, turn off the heat. Whisk for another minute and then set pan aside.

3. In the bowl of a stand mixer (or using a handheld mixer), beat together eggs, sugars, and vanilla until light and fluffy, about 3 to 4 minutes. Remove bowl from the mixer and use a small rubber spatula to fold in flour until just blended.

4. Stir in pecans and then gently fold in browned butter until completely incorporated.

5. Using a $1^1/_2$-inch-diameter scoop or a teaspoon, fill shell molds with batter until three-fourths full. Bake for 8 to 11 minutes, until madeleines puff up and spring back when gently pressed.

6. Remove pans from oven and let cool on a wire rack for 2 to 3 minutes, then invert and tap madeleines onto the rack. You may also use a small offset spatula to remove each one individually.

# SAVORY AND APPETIZER

SURE, MOST MADELEINES YOU BAKE WILL BE ON THE sweet side, but these savory takes prove the true versatility of this traditional French tea cake. From Gruyère and green chilis to crabmeat and caramelized onions, the ingredients that make these sweet treats suitable for serving with dinner is endless.

*Brie-Stuffed Madeleine Puffs (page 127)*

# GRUYÈRE AND ROSEMARY MADELEINES

**ORIGINATING FROM ITS NAMESAKE TOWN IN SWITZERLAND, GRUYÈRE IS A FLAVORFUL** hard cheese that's often described as earthy, complex, and assertive. The nutty flavor, combined with flecks of fresh aromatic rosemary, creates a madeleine that will enhance any hors d'oeuvres table.

## YIELD: 18 MADELEINES

¾ cup all-purpose flour

¼ tsp salt, plus more for sprinkling (optional)

¼ tsp freshly ground pepper

¼ tsp baking powder

10 tbsp (1¼ sticks) salted butter, room temperature, plus 4 tbsp for pans (optional)

4 large eggs, room temperature

2 tsp minced fresh rosemary

1 cup lightly packed grated Gruyère cheese

1. Place a rack in the center of the oven and preheat oven to 375°F. Coat two 12-shell pans with baking spray, or melt an additional 4 tablespoons butter and brush a little in each mold. Set pans aside.

2. In a small bowl, whisk together flour, salt, pepper, and baking powder.

3. Place butter in a 2-quart microwavable glass bowl or measuring cup. Microwave on low power for 1 to 2 minutes, until melted.

4. Let mixture cool for about 3 to 4 minutes and then add eggs, one at a time, whisking well after each addition until completely blended.

5. Whisk in flour mixture until incorporated. Stir in rosemary and cheese with a rubber spatula until just blended into batter.

6. Using a 1½-inch-diameter scoop or a teaspoon, fill shell molds with batter until almost full. Gently press batter to distribute it evenly.

7. Bake for 10 to 12 minutes, until madeleines puff up, the tops crack lightly, and the edges are golden brown.

8. Remove pans from oven and sprinkle madeleines with a little salt, if desired. Use a small offset spatula to remove each individually. You don't have to wait for these madeleines to cool before inverting the pans to remove.

# ❧ BUTTERY CORNBREAD MADELEINES ❧

**THE INSPIRATION FOR THESE MADELEINES IS THE CORNBREAD AT THE BANDERA REST-**aurant in Chicago. It is simultaneously sweet, moist, creamy, and crunchy and comes served in a hot cast-iron skillet. It's delicious with honey on top–as are these madeleines.

### YIELD: **24** MADELEINES

¾ cup shredded sharp cheddar cheese, divided

½ cup all-purpose flour

½ cup yellow cornmeal

½ tsp salt

1½ tsp baking powder

6 tbsp (¾ stick) salted butter, plus 4 tbsp for pans (optional)

½ cup granulated sugar

⅔ cup canned creamed corn

2 tbsp chopped roasted and canned green chilis

2 large eggs, room temperature

¼ cup shredded jack cheese

1. Place a rack in the center of the oven and preheat oven to 375°F. Coat two 12-shell pans with baking spray, or brush with melted butter.

2. Sprinkle ½ cup of the cheddar cheese in the prepared pans (1 teaspoon per shell). Set pans aside.

3. In a small bowl, whisk together flour, cornmeal, salt, and baking powder.

4. Place butter and sugar in a 2-quart microwavable glass bowl or measuring cup. Microwave on low power for 1 to 2 minutes, until melted. Add creamed corn and green chilis, whisking well to combine.

5. Add eggs, one at a time, whisking well after each addition until completely blended.

6. Combine the remaining cheddar and jack cheeses, stirring into batter until incorporated.

7. Stir flour mixture into batter until just incorporated. Using a scoop or a teaspoon, fill shell molds until almost full.

8. Bake for 11 to 13 minutes, until madeleines puff up and edges are golden brown.

9. Remove pans from oven and let cool on a wire rack for 2 to 3 minutes, then invert and tap madeleines onto rack. You may also use a small offset spatula to remove each one individually.

# ⤙ PESTO <u>AND</u> PINE NUT MADELEINES ⤚

**THERE'S SOMETHING ABOUT FRESH, HOMEMADE PESTO THAT FEELS NOURISHING. WHEN** added to these madeleines, it creates a savory treat that tastes great on its own and even better when paired with your favorite Italian fare.

## YIELD: **12** MADELEINES

$^1/_2$ **cup grated Parmesan cheese, divided**

**1 cup all-purpose flour**

**1 tsp salt**

$^3/_4$ **tsp baking powder**

$^1/_2$ **cup (1 stick) salted butter, room temperature, plus 2 tbsp for pan (optional)**

**2 tbsp extra-virgin olive oil**

$^1/_3$ **cup pesto, store bought or homemade**

**2 tsp granulated sugar**

**2 large eggs, room temperature**

$^1/_3$ **cup roasted unsalted pine nuts**

1. Place a rack in the center of the oven and preheat oven to 350°F. Coat one 12-shell pan with baking spray, or brush with melted butter.

2. Sprinkle $^1/_4$ cup of the Parmesan into the shell indentations, about $^1/_2$ teaspoon in each shell.

3. In a small bowl, whisk together flour, salt, and baking powder.

4. Place butter and oil in a 2-quart microwavable glass bowl or measuring cup. Microwave on low power for 1 to 2 minutes, until melted, and whisk to blend. Whisk in pesto and sugar.

5. Add eggs, one at a time, whisking well after each addition until completely blended.

6. Using a rubber spatula, stir flour mixture into batter until just incorporated, then stir in pine nuts and remaining $^1/_4$ cup Parmesan until just blended.

7. Using a $1^1/_2$-inch-diameter scoop or a teaspoon, fill shell molds with batter until almost full.

8. Bake for 11 to 13 minutes, until madeleines puff up and edges are golden brown.

9. Remove pans from oven and let cool on a wire rack for 2 to 3 minutes, then invert and tap madeleines onto the rack. You may also use a small offset spatula to remove each one individually.

# ❧ FRESH DILL AND FETA MADELEINES ❧

**DILL, A BEAUTIFUL FEATHERY HERB OFTEN USED IN GREEK CUISINE, COMPLEMENTS THE** feta in these madeleines beautifully. Serve them with Greek salad for a light but satisfying supper.

## YIELD: **12** MADELEINES

¾ cup all-purpose flour

½ tsp freshly ground black pepper

½ tsp baking powder

6 tbsp (¾ stick) salted butter, plus 2 tbsp for pan (optional)

2 large eggs, room temperature

½ cup whole milk

2 tsp granulated sugar

½ cup crumbled feta cheese

1 tbsp fresh minced dill

1. Place a rack in the center of the oven and preheat oven to 350°F. Coat one 12-shell pan with baking spray, or melt an additional 2 tablespoons butter and brush a little in each mold. Set pan aside.

2. In a small bowl, whisk together flour, pepper, and baking powder.

3. Place butter in a 2-quart microwavable glass bowl or measuring cup. Microwave on low power for 1 to 2 minutes, until melted, and whisk until smooth.

4. Let mixture cool for 3 to 4 minutes, then add eggs, one at a time, whisking well after each addition until completely blended.

5. Add milk and sugar, whisking well to blend thoroughly; stir in flour mixture.

6. Using a rubber spatula, gently stir cheese and dill into batter until just incorporated.

7. Using a 1½-inch-diameter scoop or a teaspoon, fill shell molds with batter until almost full.

8. Bake for 11 to 13 minutes, until madeleines puff up, cracks appear on top, and edges are golden brown.

9. Remove pan from oven and let cool on a wire rack for 2 to 3 minutes, then invert and tap madeleines onto rack. Or use a small offset spatula to remove them.

# ❧ CHIPOTLE MADELEINES WITH GREEN CHILIS ❧

**CHIPOTLE AND GREEN CHILIS ADD A SMOKY, SPICY FLAVOR TO THESE MADELEINES.** Feel free to increase or decrease the spiciness, depending on how much heat you like. Serve with your favorite Mexican dish.

## YIELD: **12** MADELEINES

- ¹/₂ cup all-purpose flour
- ¹/₄ cup yellow cornmeal
- ¹/₄ tsp baking powder
- ¹/₂ to ³/₄ tsp chipotle chili powder or chipotle seasoning blend
- ¹/₄ tsp salt
- ¹/₄ tsp black pepper
- 6 tbsp (³/₄ stick) salted butter, room temperature, plus 2 tbsp for pan (optional)
- 1 tbsp extra-virgin olive oil
- 2 tbsp granulated sugar
- 1 large egg, room temperature
- 4 oz chopped canned mild roasted green chilis, with liquid

1. Place a rack in the center of the oven and preheat oven to 350°F. Coat a 12-shell pan with baking spray, or melt an additional 2 tablespoons butter and brush a little in each mold. Set pan aside.

2. In a small bowl, whisk together flour, cornmeal, baking powder, chipotle seasoning, salt, and pepper.

3. Place butter, oil, and sugar in a 2-quart microwavable glass bowl or measuring cup. Microwave on low power for 1 to 2 minutes, until melted.

4. Let mixture cool for about 3 to 4 minutes and then add egg, whisking well until completely blended.

5. Whisk flour mixture into batter until incorporated. Stir in chilis with a rubber spatula.

6. Using a 1¹/₂-inch-diameter scoop or a teaspoon, fill shell molds with batter until almost full. Gently press batter to distribute it evenly.

7. Bake for 11 to 13 minutes, until madeleines puff up, small cracks appear in the tops, and the edges are golden brown.

8. Remove pan from oven and let cool on a wire rack for 2 to 3 minutes, then invert and tap madeleines onto the rack. You may also use a small offset spatula to remove each one individually.

# ❧ HERBES DE PROVENCE MADELEINES ❧

**IN THE HEAT OF SUMMER IN THE SOUTH OF FRANCE, HILLSIDES BLOOM ABUNDANTLY** with an array of herbs. Herbes de Provence typically includes rosemary, fennel, oregano, and mint. In these madeleines, the mixture infuses every bite with a delicate aroma and subtle taste.

## YIELD: 12 MADELEINES

$^1/_3$ cup plus $^1/_4$ cup shredded sharp cheddar cheese, divided

$^3/_4$ cup all-purpose flour

$^1/_2$ tsp salt

$^1/_4$ tsp freshly ground black pepper

$^3/_4$ tsp baking powder

1 tsp herbes de Provence

5 tbsp salted butter, plus 2 tbsp for pan (optional)

1 tbsp granulated sugar

3 tbsp extra-virgin olive oil

2 large eggs, room temperature

$^1/_3$ cup grated Parmesan cheese

1. Place a rack in the center of the oven and preheat oven to 350°F. Coat one 12-shell pan with baking spray, or brush with melted butter.

2. Sprinkle $^1/_4$ cup of the cheddar cheese into the shell indentations, about $^1/_2$ teaspoon in each shell. Set pans aside.

3. In a small bowl, whisk together flour, salt, pepper, baking powder, and herbes de Provence.

4. Place butter, sugar, and oil in a 2-quart microwavable glass bowl or measuring cup. Microwave on low power for 1 to 2 minutes, until melted, and whisk together to blend.

5. Let cool for 3 to 4 minutes, then add eggs, one at a time, whisking well after each addition until completely blended.

6. Add the remaining cheddar and Parmesan, and then stir in flour mixture until just incorporated.

7. Using a scoop or a teaspoon, fill shell molds until almost full. Gently press batter to distribute it evenly.

8. Bake for 10 to 12 minutes, until madeleines puff up and spring back when gently pressed.

9. Remove pan from oven and let cool on a wire rack for 2 to 3 minutes, then invert and tap madeleines onto the rack. You may also use a small offset spatula to remove each one individually.

# ✺ CRABBY MADELEINES ✺

**I OFTEN JOKE THAT NOBODY WILL BE CRABBY AFTER EATING ONE OF THESE WARM CRAB** madeleines–and yes, I get the requisite eye rolls from my teenage daughter when I do! I developed this recipe as a nod to crab, one of my favorite foods to eat at the shore every summer. The best part? No shell cracking necessary! Serve these on their own or as a side to corn chowder or your favorite seafood soup.

## YIELD: 12 TO 14 MADELEINES

5 tbsp salted butter, plus
   2 tbsp for pan (optional)

³/₄ cup all-purpose flour

³/₄ tsp baking powder

¹/₄ tsp salt

¹/₄ tsp freshly ground pepper

1 tbsp extra-virgin olive oil

¹/₂ tsp Tabasco sauce

1 large egg, room temperature

1 6-oz can crabmeat, drained
   and flaked

2 tbsp minced red onion

1 tbsp finely chopped scallions

1 tbsp grated Parmesan cheese

Paprika, to taste

1. Place a rack in the center of the oven and preheat oven to 375°F. Coat a 12-shell pan with baking spray, or melt 2 tablespoons butter and brush a little in each mold.

2. In a small bowl, whisk together flour, baking powder, salt, and pepper.

3. Place butter and oil in a 2-quart microwavable glass bowl or measuring cup. Microwave on low power for 1 to 2 minutes, until melted, and whisk well.

4. Add Tabasco and the egg, whisking until completely blended.

5. Add flour mixture, whisking until incorporated. Stir in crab, red onions, scallions, and Parmesan.

6. Using a 1¹/₂-inch-diameter scoop or a teaspoon, fill shell molds with batter until almost full. Dust lightly with paprika, if desired.

7. Bake for 10 to 12 minutes, until madeleines puff up and edges are golden brown.

8. Remove pan from oven and let cool on a wire rack for 2 to 3 minutes, then use a small offset spatula to remove each madeleine individually.

# BRIE-STUFFED MADELEINE PUFFS

**BRIE ORIGINATES IN THE NORTHERN REGION OF FRANCE CALLED SEINE-ET-MARNE, AND** it's known as the "king of cheeses." Made from cow's milk, it is rich, creamy, semisoft, and perfect for melting, especially inside madeleines. These are fantastic when served warm from the oven, and even better when paired with champagne!

## YIELD: 12 MADELEINES

- ½ cup all-purpose flour
- 1 tsp baking powder
- ⅛ tsp salt
- ⅛ tsp black pepper
- ¼ tsp minced dried rosemary
- 6 tbsp (¾ stick) butter, melted and cooled, plus 2 tbsp for pan (optional)
- 2 large eggs, room temperature
- ⅓ cup nonfat plain Greek-style yogurt
- 3 tbsp grated Parmigiano Reggiano cheese
- 12 small pieces chilled Brie, about ½ tsp each (remove rind before cutting into pieces)

1. Place a rack in the center of the oven and preheat oven to 350°F. Coat one 12-shell pan with baking spray, or melt 2 tablespoons butter and brush a little in each mold.

2. In a small bowl, whisk together flour, baking powder, salt, pepper, and rosemary.

3. Place butter in a 2-quart microwavable glass bowl or measuring cup and microwave on low for 1 to 2 minutes, until melted.

4. Let butter cool for 3 to 4 minutes and then add eggs, one at a time, whisking well after each addition until completely blended.

5. Whisk in yogurt and Parmesan cheese and then add flour mixture, stirring until completely incorporated.

6. Using a 1½-inch-diameter scoop or a teaspoon, fill shell molds with batter until almost full. Press 1 piece of Brie in the center of each madeleine.

7. Bake for 10 to 14 minutes, until madeleines puff up and edges are golden brown.

8. Remove pan from oven and let cool on a wire rack for 2 to 3 minutes, then invert and tap madeleines onto rack. Or use a small offset spatula to remove each one individually.

# ❧ CARAMELIZED ONION AND ASIAGO MADELEINES ❧

**SWEET AND MILD MEET TANGY AND ASSERTIVE IN THESE MADELEINES, WHICH ARE** mouth-wateringly good when served warm from the oven.

MADELEINES

## YIELD: **12** MADELEINES

6 tbsp (¾ stick) salted butter, divided, plus 2 tbsp for pan (optional)

1 tbsp olive oil

1 cup finely chopped onion (about 1 medium onion)

1 tsp granulated sugar

¼ tsp salt

¾ cup all-purpose flour

¼ tsp freshly ground black pepper

½ tsp baking powder

2 large eggs, room temperature

¼ cup shaved or grated Asiago cheese

1. In a medium pan, warm 1 tablespoon of the butter and oil over medium heat just until it start to bubble. Add onions, sugar, and salt and sauté until onions are light golden brown, about 5 to 6 minutes. Set aside to cool slightly.

2. Place a rack in the center of the oven and preheat oven to 350°F. Coat one 12-shell pan with baking spray, or melt an additional 2 tablespoons butter and brush a little in each mold.

3. In a small bowl, whisk together flour, pepper, and baking powder.

4. Place the remaining 5 tablespoons butter in a 2-quart microwavable glass bowl or measuring cup and microwave on low power for 1 to 2 minutes, until melted.

5. Let cool for 3 to 4 minutes, then add eggs, one at a time, whisking well after each addition until completely blended.

6. Whisk in cheese and then flour mixture until completely incorporated. Gently fold in caramelized onions.

7. Using a 1½-inch-diameter scoop or a teaspoon, fill shell molds with batter until almost full.

8. Bake for 10 to 14 minutes, until madeleines puff up and edges are golden brown.

9. Remove pan from oven and let cool on a wire rack for 2 to 3 minutes, then invert and tap madeleines onto the rack. Or use a small offset spatula to remove them.

# CHÈVRE MADELEINES WITH SCALLIONS AND SUN-DRIED TOMATOES

THESE MADELEINES WILL WOW THE GOAT CHEESE FANS IN YOUR LIFE. SCALLIONS AND sun-dried tomatoes impart an earthy flavor, and using olive oil instead of butter make these madeleines pure savory.

## YIELD: 12 TO 14 MADELEINES

¼ cup (½ stick) salted butter, 2 tbsp for pan (optional)

¾ cup all-purpose flour

2 tsp baking powder

¼ tsp salt

¼ tsp freshly ground black pepper

3 tbsp extra-virgin olive oil

2 large eggs, room temperature

3 tbsp half-and-half or whole milk

⅓ cup crumbled goat cheese

3 tbsp finely minced sun-dried tomatoes

2 tbsp finely chopped scallions

1. Place a rack in the center of the oven and preheat oven to 350°F. Coat a 12-shell pan with baking spray, or melt an additional 2 tablespoons butter and brush a little in each mold.

2. In a small bowl, whisk together flour, baking powder, salt, and pepper.

3. Place butter and oil in a 2-quart microwavable glass bowl or measuring cup. Microwave on low power for 1 to 2 minutes, until melted, and whisk well.

4. Let mixture cool for 3 to 4 minutes and then add eggs, one at a time, whisking well after each addition until completely blended.

5. Add half-and-half and whisk for 1 to 2 minutes. Stir in cheese, sun-dried tomatoes, and scallions.

6. Whisk in flour mixture until completely incorporated.

7. Using a 1½-inch-diameter scoop or a teaspoon, fill shell molds with batter until almost full.

8. Bake for 9 to 11 minutes, until madeleines puff up and edges are golden brown.

9. Remove pan from oven and let cool on a wire rack for 2 to 3 minutes. Use a small offset spatula to remove them.

# CH **6**

# INDULGENT MADELEINES

**BANANAS FOSTER, CHEESECAKE, AND MUDSLIDES,** oh my! These gussied-up madeleines are definitely dressed to impress, but you need not wait for a special occasion to serve them. They are creamy and caffeinated, minty and molten, distinctive, and–most important–delicious. These indulgences are appropriate for everything from a fancy dinner party to simply celebrating the fact that it's the weekend!

*Nonpareil Madeleines (page 146) and*
*Black and White Madeleines (page 134)*

# CHEESECAKE MADELEINES
## ❧ WITH LINGONBERRY PRESERVES ❧

**THE FRESH LEMON ZEST AND JUICE IN THESE MADELEINES ENHANCE THE FRAGRANCE** and taste of the cheesecake and pair beautifully with the tartness of the preserves. You can use any flavor of fruit preserve, but petite Swedish lingonberries are perfectly sized for madeleines. Serve on a pretty platter and sprinkle lightly with confectioners' sugar for the perfect presentation.

## YIELD: **24** MADELEINES

1 cup all-purpose flour

1 tsp baking powder

³/₄ cup (1¹/₂ sticks) unsalted butter, room temperature, plus 4 tbsp for pans (optional)

1 cup granulated sugar

¹/₃ cup cream cheese, room temperature, cut into small pieces

2 large eggs, room temperature

2 tsp freshly grated lemon zest

1 tsp fresh lemon juice

1¹/₂ tsp vanilla extract

¹/₃ cup lingonberry preserves or your favorite preserves

1. Place a rack in the center of the oven and preheat oven to 350°F. Coat two 12-shell pans with baking spray, or melt an additional 4 tablespoons butter and brush a little in each mold.

2. In a small bowl, whisk together flour and baking powder.

3. Place butter and sugar in a 2-quart microwavable glass bowl or measuring cup and microwave on low power for 1 to 2 minutes, until melted. Whisk well, either by hand or with an electric mixer, for about 3 minutes or until completely blended.

4. Add cream cheese and whisk for another 3 to 4 minutes. Then add eggs, one at a time, whisking well after each addition until completely blended.

5. Add zest, lemon juice, and vanilla, mixing well. Whisk in flour mixture until just incorporated.

6. Using a 1¹/₂-inch-diameter scoop or a teaspoon, fill shell molds with batter until almost full. Using a teaspoon or the tip of a small offset spatula, place ¹/₂ teaspoon

preserves in the center of each. There's no need to squish the preserves into the batter; it will sink during baking.

7. Bake for 10 to 12 minutes, until madeleines puff up and edges are golden brown.

8. Remove pans from oven and let cool on a wire rack for 2 to 3 minutes, then invert and tap madeleines onto the rack. You may also use a small offset spatula to remove each one individually.

"If you're afraid of butter, use cream."
—JULIA CHILD

INDULGENT MADELEINES

# ❦ BLACK AND WHITE MADELEINES ❦

**THESE DARK CHOCOLATE MADELEINES ARE ALL DRESSED UP IN MELTED WHITE CHOCOLATE.**
I like to sprinkle them with edible glitter, sprinkles, or sparkling sugar, too.

## YIELD: **12** MADELEINES OR **48** MINI MADELEINES

½ cup all-purpose flour

¼ cup unsweetened cocoa powder, either Dutch-processed or natural

6 tbsp (¾ stick) unsalted butter, room temperature, plus 2 tbsp for pans (optional)

½ cup granulated sugar

½ cup semisweet chocolate chips or ½ cup chopped bittersweet chocolate

⅓ cup water, room temperature

1 large egg, room temperature

1½ cups chopped white chocolate or white chocolate chips (not white melting disks found at hobby stores)

Decorations such as edible glitter, stars, or sprinkles (optional)

1. Place a rack in the center of the oven and preheat oven to 325°F. Coat one 12-shell pan or two mini madeleine pans with baking spray, or brush with melted butter.

2. In a small bowl, whisk together flour and cocoa powder.

3. Place butter, sugar, and chocolate chips in a 2-quart microwavable glass bowl or measuring cup and microwave on low power for 1 to 2 minutes, until melted. Add water and whisk until thoroughly melted and blended.

4. Add egg, whisking until blended. Stir in flour mixture.

5. Fill shell molds with batter until almost full.

6. Bake for 10 to 12 minutes (or 4 to 5 minutes for mini madeleines). The madeleines are done when they puff up and the dark spot in the center is almost gone.

7. Remove pans from oven and let cool on a wire rack for 2 to 3 minutes, then invert and tap madeleines onto the rack. Or use a small offset spatula to remove them.

8. Place white chocolate in a microwavable bowl and microwave on low power for 15-second increments, stirring after each, until completely melted. Stir until smooth.

9. Dip each madeleine halfway into the chocolate, scraping the flat side against the side of the bowl. Place on a waxed paper-lined sheet and let set for 15 to 20 minutes. If you are going to add glitter, stars, or sprinkles, apply them while the chocolate is still wet.

# BAKEWELL MADELEINES
## ❧ WITH DEVONSHIRE CREAM ❧

**THESE LITTLE CAKES ARE FIT FOR A QUEEN! I'VE TRANSFORMED THE BAKEWELL TART, A** traditional English dessert, into a madeleine. Serve it warm with additional pots of raspberry jam and bowls of Devonshire cream for dipping.

### YIELD: **12** MADELEINES

6 tbsp (¾ stick) unsalted butter, room temperature, plus 2 tbsp for pan (optional)

½ cup granulated sugar

2 large eggs, room temperature

1 tsp vanilla bean paste or vanilla extract

½ cup all-purpose flour

⅓ cup hazelnuts, toasted, skinned, and finely ground

⅓ cup raspberry jam

1. Place a rack in the center of the oven and preheat oven to 350°F. Coat one 12-shell pan with baking spray, or melt an additional 2 tablespoons butter and brush a little in each mold.

2. Place butter and granulated sugar in a 2-quart microwavable glass bowl or measuring cup. Microwave on low power for 1 to 2 minutes, until melted, whisking well until completely blended.

3. Let mixture cool for about 3 to 4 minutes and then add eggs, one at a time, whisking well after each addition until completely blended.

4. Add vanilla, whisking well, then add flour until incorporated into batter. Stir in hazelnuts.

5. Using a 1½-inch-diameter scoop or a teaspoon, fill shell molds with batter until almost full. Place ½ teaspoon jam in the center of each; it will sink while baking.

6. Bake for 10 to 12 minutes, until madeleines puff up and edges are golden brown.

## DEVONSHIRE CREAM

$1/2$ cup heavy whipping cream

2 to 3 tbsp confectioners' sugar, or more to taste

$3/4$ cup sour cream

**7.** While madeleines bake, make the Devonshire cream: Using a handheld mixer, whip heavy cream until soft peaks form. Add confectioners' sugar and continue whipping to blend. Add sour cream and beat mixture until light and fluffy.

**8.** Remove pans from oven and let cool on a wire rack for 2 to 3 minutes, then invert and tap madeleines onto the rack. You may also use a small offset spatula to remove each one individually. Serve warm with Devonshire cream.

# ⊱ DARK AND MINTY MADELEINES ⊱

**CONSIDERING HOW GOOD THEY TASTE, THESE MADELEINES ARE DECEPTIVELY SIMPLE** to make. A thin candy tucked in the chocolate-y cake adds a bright, bracing flavor as well as a textural contrast. I use After Eight candies because they're the thinnest, mintiest ones I've found, but feel free to experiment with others.

## YIELD: **12** MADELEINES

- ¹/₂ cup all-purpose flour
- ¹/₂ cup unsweetened cocoa powder, either Dutch-processed or natural
- 6 tbsp (³/₄ stick) unsalted butter, room temperature, plus 2 tbsp for pan (optional)
- ¹/₂ cup granulated sugar
- ¹/₂ cup bittersweet chocolate chips (such as 60 percent cacao)
- 1 large egg, room temperature
- ¹/₃ cup warm water
- ¹/₂ tsp peppermint extract

1. Place a rack in the center of the oven and preheat oven to 325°F. Coat one 12-shell pan with baking spray, or melt an additional 2 tablespoons butter and brush a little in each mold.

2. In a small bowl, whisk together flour and cocoa powder.

3. Place butter, sugar, and chocolate in a 2-quart micro-wavable glass bowl or measuring cup. Microwave on low power for 1 to 2 minutes and then stir with a whisk until smooth. If ingredients are not melted, microwave for 15-second intervals, stirring after each, until smooth.

4. Let mixture cool for about 3 to 4 minutes and then add egg, whisking well until completely blended. Add water and extract, whisking thoroughly. The mixture should be thick and shiny.

5. Using a 1¹/₂-inch-diameter scoop or a teaspoon, fill shell molds with batter until almost full.

6. Bake for 10 to 12 minutes, until madeleines puff up and the dark spot in the center of each is almost gone.

12 thin mints small enough to fit the shell molds (or 6 After Eights cut in half)

¼ cup confectioners' sugar (optional)

**7.** Remove pan from oven and place a mint candy onto each warm madeleine, pressing it slightly. It will melt into the madeleine. Let pan cool on a wire rack for 3 to 4 minutes, then use a small offset spatula to remove each madeleine individually. If desired, sift confectioners' sugar over the ridged side of the madeleines before serving.

"Cooking is like love. It should be entered into with abandon or not at all."

—HARRIET VAN HORNE

# ❧ BANANAS FOSTER MADELEINES ❧

**IF I MUST HAVE A CHOCOLATE-FREE DESSERT, I'LL CHOOSE THIS ONE EVERY TIME.** Created by layering a sweet sauce of brown sugar, butter, and sliced bananas over vanilla bean–flecked ice cream, bananas Foster is also often set alight after the rum is added. For this adaptation, vanilla madeleines are served under or alongside vanilla ice cream and topped with a brown sugar syrup. Feel free to spoon some rum over top and ignite it for a spectacular presentation.

## YIELD: **12** MADELEINES

¹/₂ cup all-purpose flour

¹/₄ tsp salt

¹/₄ tsp baking powder

¹/₂ tsp freshly grated nutmeg

6 tbsp (³/₄ stick) unsalted butter, room temperature, plus 2 tbsp for pan (optional)

¹/₂ cup dark brown sugar, packed

1 large egg, room temperature

¹/₂ medium, ripe banana, mashed (about ¹/₃ cup mashed)

¹/₂ tsp vanilla extract

Vanilla ice cream, for serving

1. Place a rack in the center of the oven and preheat oven to 350°F. Coat one 12-shell pan with baking spray, or brush with melted butter.

2. In a small bowl, whisk together flour, salt, baking powder, and nutmeg.

3. Place butter and brown sugar in a 2-quart microwavable glass bowl or measuring cup. Microwave on low power for 1 to 2 minutes, until melted, and then whisk the mixture until smooth.

4. Let mixture cool for about 3 to 4 minutes and then whisk in egg until completely blended. Add mashed banana and extract, whisking thoroughly to combine.

5. Using a 1¹/₂-inch-diameter scoop or a teaspoon, fill shell molds with batter until almost full.

6. Bake for 10 to 12 minutes, until madeleines puff up and edges are golden brown.

7. Remove pan from oven and let cool on a wire rack for 2 to 3 minutes, then invert and tap madeleines onto the rack and let cool completely. You may also use a small offset spatula to remove each one individually.

## BROWN SUGAR SYRUP

¹/₄ cup (¹/₂ stick) unsalted butter

1 cup dark brown sugar, packed

¹/₂ tsp ground cinnamon

1¹/₂ medium bananas, sliced into
¹/₄-inch rounds

2 tbsp dark rum (optional)

## TO SERVE

1. Place butter, brown sugar, and cinnamon in a medium saucepan over low heat, stirring constantly to dissolve sugar. Once sugar has dissolved, add sliced bananas and cook, gently stirring, until bananas are soft, about 2 to 4 minutes.

2. Turn off heat. Stir in rum, if using.

3. Place one or two madeleines in a bowl with a scoop of vanilla ice cream and drizzle brown sugar syrup over top.

# ❧ MUDSLIDE MADELEINES ❧

**BEING EXCESSIVELY FOND OF CHOCOLATE, I HAVE A THICK FOLDER FULL OF RECIPES** for decadent mudslide cookies. My favorite is the creation of master pastry chef Jacques Torres (a.k.a. Mr. Chocolate), owner of the Jacques Torres chocolate factories in New York City. Smushed into each of his mudslide cookies are three kinds of chocolate as well as toasted walnuts. I kept that chocolate-packed tradition alive in these madeleines.

## YIELD: **24** MADELEINES

⅓ cup all-purpose flour

1¼ tsp baking powder

¼ tsp salt

16 oz bittersweet chocolate (such as 60 percent cacao), finely chopped, divided

3 oz unsweetened chocolate, chopped

¼ cup (½ stick) unsalted butter, room temperature, plus 4 tbsp for pans (optional)

1 cup granulated sugar

3 eggs, room temperature

¾ cup toasted walnuts, chopped

1. Place a rack in the center of the oven and preheat oven to 350°F. Coat two 12-shell pans with baking spray, or melt an additional 4 tablespoons butter and brush a little in each mold.

2. In a small bowl, whisk together flour, baking powder, and salt.

3. Place half the bittersweet chocolate and the unsweetened chocolate in a microwavable bowl. Microwave on low power for 1 to 2 minutes and whisk until smooth. If chocolate is not melted, microwave for 15-second intervals, stirring after each, until smooth. Set aside. (Alternatively, you can combine these ingredients in the top of a double boiler over simmering water and stir with a whisk until smooth, then remove from heat.)

4. Place butter and sugar in the bowl of a stand mixer (or a 2-quart glass bowl or measuring cup if you're using a hand mixer). Cream until light and fluffy, 3 to 4 minutes. Add eggs, one at a time, beating well on low, then medium-high speed after each addition, about 3 to 4 minutes. The mixture should be light and fluffy.

5. Mix in flour mixture on low speed until combined. Add melted chocolate. Finally, stir in the remaining bittersweet chocolate and walnuts.

6. Using a 1$^1$/$_2$-inch-diameter scoop or a teaspoon, fill shell molds with batter until almost full. Gently press batter to distribute it evenly.

7. Bake for 9 to 12 minutes, until madeleines puff up and small cracks appear.

8. Remove pans from oven and let cool on a wire rack for 2 to 3 minutes, then invert and tap madeleines onto the rack. You may also use a small offset spatula to remove each one individually. Let cool completely.

---

MADELEINE MUST-HAVE:

◇◇◇◇◇◇◇ **CHOCOLATE** ◇◇◇◇◇◇◇

Tempted to buy bargain chocolate? Keep in mind that flavor depends on the quality of the chocolate you use. Buy the best you can afford to make the most delicious madeleines.

# ⸙ HAZELNUT AND FRANGELICO MADELEINES ⸙

**THE MAGIC COMBINATION OF HAZELNUTS AND CHOCOLATE GETS A BOOZY BOOST** from Frangelico, a hazelnut liqueur made in the northern Italian region of the Piedmont. The hints of herbs, vanilla, and cocoa infused in Frangelico work perfectly in these madeleines to create a light, nutty, flavorful cakelet.

### YIELD: **24** MADELEINES

¾ cup (1½ sticks) unsalted butter, plus 4 tbsp for pans (optional)

1 cup granulated sugar

2 large eggs, room temperature

1 tsp vanilla bean paste or vanilla extract

2 tsp Frangelico, other hazelnut liqueur, or water

1 cup all-purpose flour

1½ cups toasted hazelnuts, finely chopped, divided

8 oz dark or semisweet chocolate, chopped

1. Place a rack in the center of the oven and preheat oven to 325°F. Coat two 12-shell pans with baking spray, or melt an additional 4 tablespoons butter and brush a little in each mold.

2. Place butter and sugar in a 2-quart microwavable glass bowl or measuring cup. Microwave on low power for 1 to 2 minutes, until melted, then whisk until completely blended.

3. Let mixture cool for about 3 to 4 minutes and then whisk in add eggs, one at a time, until completely blended.

4. Add vanilla, whisking well, and then add liqueur.

5. Stir in flour until just blended and then ⅓ cup of the hazelnuts until incorporated.

6. Using a 1½-inch-diameter scoop or a teaspoon, fill shell molds with batter until almost full.

7. Bake for 10 to 12 minutes, until madeleines puff up and edges are golden brown.

8. Remove pans from oven and let cool on a wire rack for 2 to 3 minutes, then invert and tap madeleines onto the rack. You may also use a small offset spatula to remove each one individually.

## TO DECORATE

1. While the madeleines are cooling, place chocolate in a microwavable bowl. Microwave on low power for 1 to 2 minutes and then whisk until smooth. If chocolate is not melted, microwave for 15-second intervals, stirring after each, until smooth.

2. Line a cookie sheet or large wire rack with waxed paper. Place the remaining hazelnuts in a wide shallow dish. Holding a madeleine on its long side, dip it halfway into the warm chocolate and gently scrape the flat side along the edge of the bowl to remove excess chocolate. Next, dip it into the nuts to cover the chocolate. Place madeleines onto waxed paper and let chocolate set for 30 to 60 minutes.

# ❧ NONPAREIL MADELEINES ❧

**IN FRANCE, NONPAREILS—WHOSE LITERAL TRANSLATION IS "WITHOUT PARALLEL"—ARE** traditionally used as decorative pastry centerpieces. (In the U.S., they are sometimes also called snowies, jazzies, or sno-caps.) They also make gorgeous madeleines. Whether you use classic white, snazzy silver, or multicolored nonpareils, you'll have fun dipping and decorating these madeleines—and delighting in the *ooobs* and *ahbb*s when you serve them at your next party.

MADELEINES

## YIELD: 12 MADELEINES

- ³/₄ cup all-purpose flour
- ¹/₄ cup unsweetened cocoa powder, either Dutch-processed or natural
- ¹/₈ tsp salt
- ¹/₂ cup (1 stick) butter, plus 2 tbsp for pan (optional)
- ³/₄ cup granulated sugar
- 2 eggs
- 1¹/₂ cups semisweet chocolate chips, divided
- ¹/₂ cup nonpareils

1. Place a rack in the center of the oven and preheat oven to 350°F. Coat one 12-shell pan with baking spray, or melt an additional 2 tablespoons butter and brush a little in each mold.

2. In a small bowl, whisk together flour, cocoa powder, and salt.

3. Place butter and sugar in a 2-quart microwavable glass bowl or measuring cup and microwave on low power for 1 to 2 minutes, until melted. Whisk well, either by hand or with an electric mixer, for about 3 minutes or until completely blended.

4. Let mixture cool for about 3 to 4 minutes and then add eggs, one at a time, whisking well after each addition. Stir in ¹/₃ cup of the chocolate chips until incorporated.

5. Using a 1¹/₂-inch-diameter scoop or a teaspoon, fill shell molds with batter until almost full.

6. Bake for 10 to 12 minutes, until madeleines puff up and edges are golden brown.

**7.** Remove pans from oven and let cool on a wire rack for 2 to 3 minutes, then invert and tap madeleines onto the rack. You may also use a small offset spatula to remove each one individually.

## TO DECORATE

**1.** While the madeleines are cooling, place the remaining chocolate chips in a microwavable bowl. Microwave on low power for 30 seconds, stirring with a whisk until smooth. If chocolate is not melted, microwave for 15-second intervals, stirring after each, until smooth.

**2.** Place the nonpareils in a wide shallow dish. Line a cookie sheet or large wire rack with a piece of waxed paper. Dip the flat side of each madeleine into the warm chocolate and gently scrape it along the side of the bowl to remove excess. Dip into the nonpareils to cover the chocolate. Place madeleines coated side up on the waxed paper and let set for 30 to 60 minutes.

If dipping the flat side of your madeleines into the chocolate is getting too messy, spread the melted chocolate onto the flat side with an offset spatula. You want a neat, thin chocolate coating—just enough to hold the nonpareils in place.

# ❧ HARRIETT'S MADELEINE TIRAMISU ❧

**BAKING SKILLS SEEM TO RUN IN MY FAMILY, AND MY SISTER HARRIETT DEFINITELY GOT** the gene. She created this tiramisu adaptation that has it all: a not-too-sweet coffee flavor and a creamy, cakey texture. Serve these madeleines in a glass trifle bowl for a spectacular take on traditional tiramisu.

### YIELD: **24** MADELEINES

1 cup all-purpose flour

¼ tsp baking powder

¼ tsp salt

1 tbsp instant espresso powder

3 large eggs, room temperature

½ cup granulated sugar

1 tsp vanilla extract

8 tbsp (1 stick) unsalted butter, melted and cooled, plus 4 tbsp for pans (optional)

1. In a small bowl, whisk together flour, baking powder, salt, and espresso powder.

2. Place eggs, sugar, and vanilla in the large bowl of a stand mixer fitted with the paddle attachment. Beat on medium speed until the batter is light and fluffy, about 7 minutes. Using a rubber spatula, gently fold in the flour mixture until combined, then stir in the melted butter and mix by hand until evenly blended.

3. Cover the bowl and refrigerate at least 2 hours or overnight.

4. When ready to bake, place a rack in the center of the oven and preheat oven to 350°F. Coat two 12-shell pans with baking spray, or melt 4 tablespoons of butter and brush into each mold.

5. Using a 1½-inch-diameter scoop or a teaspoon, fill shell molds until almost full.

6. Bake for 8 to 11 minutes, until madeleines puff up and the edges are golden brown. You can also insert a cake tester in the middle; the madeleines are done when it comes out clean.

## FILLINGS AND TOPPINGS

$^1/_2$ cup espresso or very strong coffee, room temperature

1 tbsp vanilla extract

$^1/_4$ cup granulated sugar, divided

$^1/_4$ cup sweet Marsala wine, divided, or more to taste

4 large egg yolks

8 oz mascarpone cheese

$^3/_4$ cup heavy cream

1 3.5-ounce 72% dark chocolate bar, grated

7. Remove pans from the oven and let cool on a wire rack for 2 to 3 minutes, then invert and tap madeleines onto the rack. You may also use a small offset spatula to remove each one individually.

## TO ASSEMBLE

1. Make the espresso syrup: In a small bowl, mix espresso, vanilla, 1 tablespoon sugar, and 2 tablespoons of the Marsala.

2. Make the mascarpone filling: In a medium bowl set in a double boiler, whisk together egg yolks, 3 tablespoons sugar, and 2 tablespoons Marsala (or simmering water). Stir constantly until mixture has thickened and tripled in volume. Remove from heat and stir in the mascarpone until well blended. Cool for 5 minutes.

3. In another medium bowl, whip heavy cream using a hand mixer until stiff peaks form. Gently fold the whipped cream into the mascarpone mixture until smooth.

4. To construct the tiramisu, dip half of each madeleine into the espresso syrup. Line the bottom and sides of a 2-quart trifle-style glass bowl with the espresso-dipped madeleines. Spread half the mascarpone filling over the soaked madeleines and sprinkle with half the grated chocolate. Repeat with the remaining madeleines.

5. Cover tightly with plastic wrap and refrigerate for at least 4 hours (or overnight).

# ⟡ NIGHTCAP MADELEINES WITH AFFOGATO ⟡

**SERVING GRAND MARNIER MADELEINES ALONGSIDE A TRADITIONAL AFFOGATO—VANILLA** ice cream with a shot of hot espresso poured over top—is a magical pairing.

MADELEINES

## YIELD: **12 MADELEINES**

6 tbsp (³⁄₄ stick) unsalted butter, room temperature, plus 4 tbsp for pan (optional)

¹⁄₂ cup granulated sugar

1 large egg, room temperature

¹⁄₂ teaspoon vanilla extract

1 tsp freshly grated orange zest

1 tbsp and 1 teaspoon Grand Marnier Liqueur (or frozen orange juice concentrate), plus additional for serving

¹⁄₂ cup flour

1 pint vanilla bean ice cream

¹⁄₄ cup good-quality espresso for each madeleine you're serving

1. Place rack in the center of the oven and preheat to 350°F. Coat one 12-shell pan with baking spray, or melt 4 table-spoons of butter and brush into each mold.

2. Place butter and sugar in a 2-quart microwavable glass bowl or measuring cup. Microwave on low for 1 to 2 minutes, until melted, and then whisk the mixture until smooth. If more melting is needed, microwave at 15-second intervals, stirring after each until smooth.

3. Let mixture cool for about 3 to 4 minutes and then add eggs, one at a time, whisking well after each addition. Add the vanilla, zest, and liqueur, whisking thoroughly. Stir in the flour until just combined.

4. Using a scoop or a teaspoon, fill shell molds with batter until almost full. Gently press batter to distribute it.

5. Bake for 9 to 12 minutes, until madeleines puff up and edges are golden brown.

6. Remove pans from the oven and let cool on a wire rack for 2 to 3 minutes, then invert and tap madeleines onto the rack. Let cool completely.

## TO ASSEMBLE

1. Place one or two madeleines in each bowl with a scoop of ice cream.

2. Pour ¹⁄₄ cup espresso over the ice cream and madeleines. Spoon more Grand Marnier on top (optional).

# CH 7
# ALL IN THE PRESENTATION

**MADELEINES ARE SO DELICIOUS, IT DOESN'T REALLY** matter how you serve them. But if you want to go all out and give your madeleines an especially pretty presentation, this chapter has all the sides, dips, and serving suggestions you need.

*Tabitian Vanilla Bean Madeleines (page 34)*

# ❧ CHOCOLATE GLAZE ❧

**MELTED DARK, MILK, OR WHITE CHOCOLATE MAKES A CLASSIC GLAZE THAT'S PERFECT** for dipping, coating, or drizzling over madeleines.

## YIELD: 1 CUP

2 cups dark, milk, or white chocolate chips, or 12 ounces chopped chocolate

1. Place chocolate in a 2-quart microwavable glass bowl or measuring cup and microwave on low for 1 to 2 minutes, until melted. Stir until smooth. If more melting is needed, microwave at 15-second intervals until smooth.

2. Dip each madeleine in the melted chocolate and let set on a parchment-lined baking sheet.

MADELEINES

## ◇◇◇◇◇◇ VARIATION ◇◇◇◇◇◇

Here's a swanky presentation that uses all three kinds of chocolate. Melt each chocolate separately, as directed in step 1. Dip a madeleine two-thirds of the way into melted dark chocolate and let set as in step 2. Next, dip the madeleine into the melted milk chocolate, leaving some of the dark chocolate showing, and let set. Lastly, dip the madeleine into melted white chocolate, leaving the first two chocolates showing. Tastes great and looks smashing!

# ❧ MAPLE WHIPPED CREAM ❧

**RICH, HEAVY CREAM AND REAL MAPLE SYRUP ARE WHIPPED TOGETHER TO CREATE AN** easy side for your favorite madeleines. I love serving this topping with Francie's Apple Madeleines (page 64) or Mapley Granola Madeleines (page 61). I've even been known to add a drop to a steaming cup of coffee.

## YIELD: ABOUT **2** CUPS

1 cup cold heavy cream

¼ cup grade B maple syrup

1. Chill the bowl and whip attachment of your stand mixer by placing them in the freezer for 15 to 20 minutes.

2. Pour cream into the bowl and beat on medium until soft peaks form, about 3 to 4 minutes.

3. Drizzle in maple syrup, beating until the whipped cream is light and fluffy, another minute or so.

"If you are a chef, no matter how good a chef
you are, it's not good cooking for yourself; the joy
is in cooking for others. It's the same with music."

—WILL.I.AM

# ❧ CHOCOLATE-HAZELNUT BUTTER ❧

NUTELLA IS CONSIDERED BY SOME TO BE A DIVINELY INSPIRED PART OF LIFE, AND I must admit that I wholeheartedly agree. There are literally hundreds of recipes for this sublime and addictive chocolate-y spread. I prefer dark chocolate instead of milk chocolate, and I use all hazelnuts instead of a combination of hazelnuts and almonds. Whatever you do, just be sure to use fresh, toasted hazelnuts with the skins removed. That will ensure a smooth texture and perfectly nutty flavor.

MADELEINES

## YIELD: ABOUT 4 CUPS

2¹/₂ cups hazelnuts, toasted and skinned

¹/₄ cup granulated sugar

16 oz bittersweet chocolate, semisweet chocolate, or a combination of both, coarsely chopped

8 tbsp (1 stick) unsalted butter, room temperature

1 cup heavy cream

1. In a food processor, grind hazelnuts and sugar to a paste, about 1 minute.

2. Place chocolate in a clean, dry microwavable bowl and microwave on low for 1¹/₂ minutes. Stir, making sure to scrape the bottom of the bowl. Continue microwaving for 30-second intervals, stirring after each, until chocolate is melted and smooth. Watch carefully so it doesn't burn.

3. Place melted chocolate in a medium bowl and whisk in butter until smooth. Add cream, whisking to blend thoroughly.

4. Add hazelnut paste and whisk until smooth.

5. Pour into a container or individual jars and cover. The hazelnut butter will thicken as it cools.

# ❖ WHIPPED HONEY BUTTER ❖

**THIS SIMPLE SPREAD COMPLEMENTS MOST VARIETIES OF MADELEINES AND KEEPS WELL** refrigerated in a covered container. For variety, consider adding a pinch or two of cinnamon, grated lemon or orange peel, or toasted pecans.

## YIELD: ABOUT 2 CUPS

1 lb (4 sticks) unsalted butter, room temperature

1/3 cup honey, your favorite flavor

1/2 tsp vanilla bean paste or vanilla extract

Pinch salt, if desired

1. Place butter in a stand mixer and beat on medium speed for 2 to 3 minutes.

2. Add honey, vanilla, and salt and beat for another 3 or 4 minutes, until fluffy and smooth.

3. Spoon into a container with a tight-fitting lid. The honey butter will keep refrigerated for several weeks.

---

MADELEINE MUST-HAVE:

## PRESENTATION

Dress up a dozen with one of these packaging ideas:

· Fill a small new plastic beach pail with madeleines. Wrap the pail in clear cellophane and tie with twine.

· Place several mini madeleines onto a large, flat scallop baking shell. Arrange with a few pieces of rock candy, wrap in cellophane, and tie with nylon cord.

· Pour about 1/2 inch of white sparkling sugar into the bottom of a clear glass jar, add a few pieces of rock candy, and fill with a variety of mini madeleines. Screw on the lid and wrap the jar in aqua cellophane. Tie the cellophane with raffia and attach real shells to each end.

· Line a decorative gift box with colorful waxed tissue paper and fill with madeleines. Wrap it in raffia for a simple finishing touch.

# ❧ CANDIED VIOLETS ❧

**THIS SPRINGTIME PROJECT CAPTURES THE COLORS AND FRESHNESS OF THE SEASON.**
Place a few of these edible flowers on a platter of madeleines and you've got a conversation starter—
and a beautiful sweet treat! Just remember to use only homegrown violets that you know have not
been sprayed or treated with toxic substances.

## YIELD: 20 TO 30 VIOLETS

2 cups granulated or superfine
sugar

2 to 3 egg whites, placed as is in
another bowl, not whisked or
beaten

Freshly picked violets (not
African violets), unwashed
and with stems intact

1. Place sugar in a shallow bowl. Place egg whites in a separate bowl; do not whisk or beat them. Line a baking sheet
   with parchment or waxed paper.

2. Dip each violet into the egg white. Alternatively, you can
   use a small paintbrush to coat.

3. Dip each flower into the sugar, coating it completely.

4. Lay violets on the baking sheet; allow to dry thoroughly
   for 24 hours. Store in an airtight container for up to a
   month.

# ❖ ORANGETTES ❖

**HOMEMADE ORANGETTES OWE THEIR ALLURE TO THE CONTRAST OF GOOD-QUALITY** bittersweet chocolate and fresh, sweet oranges. These are so much better than the standard candies– plus they're surprisingly easy to make. For a variation, try dipping lemons, limes, or tangerines and in white chocolate.

## YIELD: 10 TO 12 SERVINGS

1¹/₂ cups water

1¹/₂ cups granulated sugar

3 to 4 thick-skinned organic navel oranges, rinsed and dried

1 lb bittersweet chocolate, chopped

1. Make a simple syrup by placing water and sugar in a saucepan over high heat. Boil until sugar has dissolved, using a wooden spoon to scrape down the sugar crystals on the side of the pan. Reduce heat to low.

2. Cut the tops and bottoms off the oranges. Score the oranges from "pole to pole" and then remove the peel and slice it into ¹/₂-inch strips.

3. Place peels into the hot syrup and return liquid to a boil. Reduce heat to low and simmer for 45 to 60 minutes.

4. Drain peels and arrange, separated, on a cookie sheet lined with foil. Let air-dry overnight.

5. Place chocolate in a 2-quart microwavable glass bowl or measuring cup and heat on low for 1 minute. Stir and repeat, heating at 30-second intervals and whisking after each, until melted chocolate is smooth.

6. Dip each peel two-thirds of the way into the chocolate. You can also dunk each one entirely. Place peels onto a parchment- or foil-lined baking sheet until chocolate sets.

# CLASSIC POTS DE CRÈME AU CHOCOLAT

**A FRIEND IN SAN FRANCISCO GAVE ME THIS RECIPE MANY YEARS AGO. HE OFFERED THIS** phenomenal chocolate delight at his small restaurant, serving it in classic porcelain cups with little covers.

## YIELD: 8 SERVINGS

2 cups light cream

4 oz bittersweet chocolate, chopped fine

2 tbsp granulated sugar

Pinch salt

6 large egg yolks, stirred lightly

1 1/2 tsp vanilla extract

1. Preheat oven to 325°F.

2. Rinse a small heavy-bottomed saucepan with cold water, and place 1 1/2 cups of the cream in it over low heat. Stir often to prevent skin forming on the surface.

3. Meanwhile, place the remaining 1/2 cup cream and the chocolate in the top of a double boiler set over medium heat. Stir to melt.

4. When small bubbles appear around the edges of the pot of cream, it is scalded. (You can also use a thermometer to judge when the cream is scalded; it will reach 180°F.) Stir in sugar and salt and then remove from heat. Slowly add hot cream to the chocolate mixture, stirring constantly.

5. While stirring, add yolks little by little to blend completely. Whisk in vanilla.

6. Return mixture to the top portion of the double boiler and stir constantly with a rubber spatula for 3 to 4 minutes.

7. Pour mixture through a fine strainer and then pour into soufflé dishes, leaving a bit of room at the top.

8. Place dishes in a shallow baking pan and add water to the pan until it reaches halfway up the sides of the dishes. Cover the pan with foil and bake in the center of the oven for 22 minutes. Carefully remove from the oven and place on a wire rack to cool. Refrigerate until ready to serve. Serve with whipped cream and a candied violet.

# ❧ EASY, MAGICAL, NO-CHURN ICE CREAM ❧

**I'VE GOT NIGELLA LAWSON TO THANK FOR THESE DELECTABLE SCOOPS OF NO-CHURN ICE** cream. I've used her formula as inspiration for these recipes. See the basic recipe directions first, then get creative with add-ins to create all kinds of delicious flavors.

## YIELD: 4 TO 6 SERVINGS

1¼ cups heavy whipping cream, chilled

⅔ cup sweetened condensed milk

1. Place all ingredients in the bowl of a stand mixer or hand mixer and, using the whisk attachment, beat until light and fluffy, about 7 to 8 minutes. The more air whipped into the mixture, the smoother the ice cream.

2. With a rubber spatula, transfer mixture to a container and cover the surface with plastic wrap and then foil, wrapping tightly. Freeze for at least 6 hours and up to overnight.

## ◇◇◇◇◇◇ FLAVORS TO TRY ◇◇◇◇◇◇

**For Vanilla Ice Cream:**

2 teaspoons vanilla bean paste or vanilla extract

1 to 2 tablespoons Bourbon (optional)

**For Coffee Ice Cream:**

2 tablespoons instant espresso powder

2 tablespoons Kahlúa or other coffee liqueur, or strong brewed coffee

# ❧ ICE CREAM SANDWICHES ❧

**HERE'S AN IMPRESSIVE PRESENTATION: MAKE YOUR OWN ICE CREAM SANDWICHES!**
The trick is to make sure your ice cream is slightly softened so that it's easier to spread.

## YIELD: 1 SANDWICH

1 tbsp slightly melted ice
   cream or gelato, any flavor,
   or to taste

2 madeleines or mini
   madeleines, chilled

Chocolate chips, grated citrus
   rind, toasted nuts, sprinkles,
   or any other ice cream topping
   imaginable (optional)

Spread a layer of ice cream between two madeleines. Roll the edges of the ice cream into topping, if using. Freeze for at least 2 hours before serving.

MADELEINES

# ❧ CRÈME CARAMEL ❧

SMOOTH, SILKY, AND CREAMY, CRÈME CARAMEL IS ALSO COMMONLY KNOWN AS FLAN.
The more whipped cream you substitute for milk, the richer it will be.

## YIELD: 6 SERVINGS

### CARAMEL SAUCE

²/₃ cup granulated sugar

¹/₃ cup water

### CUSTARD

2¹/₂ cups whole milk, or
substitute whipping cream
for up to half the milk

1 whole vanilla bean, split
lengthwise, or 1¹/₂
teaspoons vanilla bean
paste or extract

¹/₂ cup granulated sugar

3 large eggs

3 egg yolks

1. Preheat oven to 325°F. Place 6 small soufflé cups into a 9-by-13-inch pan.

2. Combine sugar and water in a heavy-bottomed saucepan over medium heat. Swirl the mixture until dissolved. Continue cooking until the syrup turns a light brown.

3. Remove from heat and quickly pour into the soufflé cups. Swirl syrup to coat the sides and bottom. Set aside.

4. Place milk in a saucepan. If using a vanilla pod, scrape out the seeds and add them and the pod to the milk. Bring to just under a simmer and turn off heat. Remove pod.

5. In a stand mixer, beat sugar, eggs, yolks (and vanilla, if using extract) until light and fluffy, about 5 to 6 minutes. In a thin stream, pour hot milk into the egg mixture, continuing to beat another 2 to 3 minutes.

6. Strain through a fine-mesh sieve into the soufflé cups.

7. Pour hot water halfway up the sides of the soufflé cups in the pan and bake for 30 to 40 minutes, until the center of the custard just becomes firm. Do not overbake. Remove the cups to a cooling rack and let cool to room temperature. Chill for several hours.

8. To unmold, run a sharp knife around the custard inside the cup. Invert a plate on top of the soufflé cup and turn both over. Shake to release the custard onto the plate.

# ❧ PEPPERMINT-ICED CHOCOLATE MOUSSE ❧

**STUFFED BITTERSWEET CHOCOLATE MINT SEASHELLS (PAGE 80) ARE A PERFECT MATCH** for this mousse if you want a super-minty dessert.

## YIELD: **12** SERVINGS

5 oz semisweet or dark chocolate, chopped

1 tbsp unsalted butter

3 large eggs, separated

2 tbsp cream, half-and-half, or whole milk

$1/2$ tsp peppermint extract

1 tbsp plus 1 teaspoon granulated sugar

Additional whipped cream for serving (optional)

1. Place chocolate and butter in a 2-quart microwavable glass bowl or measuring cup. Microwave on low power for 30-second intervals, stirring after each, until melted.

2. Add egg yolks, blending well until smooth. Whisk in cream or milk completely, followed by peppermint extract.

3. Whip the egg whites in a clean mixing bowl on low, gradually adding the sugar one teaspoon at a time. Gradually increase the speed to medium and beat until the whites have formed soft peaks. Do not overwhip. Gently fold into the chocolate mixture.

4. Using a small scoop, fill shot glasses with mousse. Cover with plastic wrap and arrange in a 9-by-13-inch pan to freeze for at least 6 hours or overnight.

5. Serve with a dollop of whipped cream.

# ❧ CHOCOLATE FONDUE ❧

**NOTHING IS BETTER THAN AN ARRAY OF MINI MADELEINES AND FRESH SEASONAL FRUITS** dipped, dunked, and splashed into warm melted chocolate. Chocolate fondue at its most basic is a ganache: good-quality chocolate melted with cream. For a more distinct chocolate flavor, substitute milk for the cream. A small amount of butter creates a smoother texture and milder flavor. Also feel free to mix in your favorite liqueur. Nutella is another add-in that never gets any complaints!

## YIELD: 6 TO 8 SERVINGS

½ cup heavy cream
(or whole milk)

10 oz good-quality bittersweet,
semisweet, or milk chocolate

1 to 2 tbsp unsalted butter

Place all ingredients in a 2-quart microwavable glass bowl or measuring cup and microwave on low power at 30-second intervals, stirring after each. Transfer chocolate to a fondue pot or mini slow cooker set on low heat.

## ◇◇◇◇◇ HOW TO FONDUE IT ◇◇◇◇◇

A fondue pot will keep chocolate melted just below 120°F; a mini slow cooker also does the trick. No fondue forks in the kitchen? Grab your quirkiest swizzle sticks, bamboo skewers, or seafood forks. Along with serving mini madeleines with the fondue, I offer a variety of fresh fruit—whatever's in season is best. You could also place small bowls of toasted chopped nuts, toasted coconut, or even flax and sunflower seeds to dip into after a chocolate dunk. Bowls of whipped cream—plain or flavored—are a natural accompaniment. Chocolate fondue is definitely a "more is better" kind of thing!

# ❧ BAKER'S CHOICE ❧

**MOST OF THE RECIPES IN THIS BOOK ARE READY FOR PERSONALIZATION THROUGH THE** addition of nuts, chocolate, or other "baker's choice" items. Mix one or more of these ingredients into your next batch. Or, spread freshly baked madeleines with an icing, nut butter, or chocolate glaze and dip into one (or more) of these ingredients.

Toasted coconut, shredded or flaked

Toffee crunch

Mini cinnamon chips

Mint chips

White chocolate chips

Toasted, chopped nuts and seeds

Granola

Nonpareils

Sanding sugars

Edible glitter

Sparkling white sugar

Sugar pearls

Candy canes (chopped)

Exotic chocolate bars (chopped)

Almond paste, pistachio paste, nut pralines

Candied fruits: cherries, orange, lemon, lime, pineapple, maple sugar

Crystallized ginger

Chopped dates and figs

Icing, nut butter, or chocolate glaze (for dipped madeleines)

MADELEINE MUST-HAVE:
## ◇◇◇◇◇◇ DESSERT BUFFET ◇◇◇◇◇◇

Mix and match madeleines with your favorite dips, sauces, or accompaniments for a spectacular party finale. Place baskets of freshly baked mini madeleines around a turntable holding small bowls of honey, Nutella, grated chocolate, toasted nuts, pumpkin seeds, maple cream, apple butter, hot fudge sauce, and whipped cream. Or try little pots of jams, jellies, marmalades, and dishes of fresh berries or cut fruit. On the savory spectrum are sunflower seed butter, hazelnut butter, praline pastes, cream cheeses, ricotta, and yogurt.

# ❧ RESOURCES ❧

Exploring the wide world of cookware, colorful serving ware, decorating supplies, and artisan food products is part of the fun. Here are a few of my favorite places to start.

## ANTHROPOLOGIE
www.anthropologie.com
Cookware, baking supplies, and stylish serving ware.

## BEANILLA TRADING COMPANY
www.beanilla.com
888-261-3384
Fantastic selection of vanilla products: beans, powders, pastes, infusions, and more.

## BERYL'S CAKE DECORATING AND PASTRY SUPPLIES
www.beryls.com
800-488-2749
Chocolate "river rocks" and "beach pebbles," dragées of all kinds, edible glitter and diamonds.

## BROWN COOKIE
www.browncookie.com
855-888-0288
Bakeware and cookware for the home chef. Round shell-shaped madeleine pans, utensils, sprinkles, glitters, flavorings.

## CRATE AND BARREL
www.crateandbarrel.com
An ever-changing selection of stylish pans, bowls, utensils, and serving ware for baking and more.

## FANTES KITCHEN SHOP
www.fantes.com
800-443-2683
Enormous selection of madeleine pans: round shell-shaped nonstick madeleine pans, nutmeg graters, utensils, pots de crème cups, lots more fun stuff.

## KEREKES BAKERY AND RESTAURANT EQUIPMENT INC.
www.bakedeco.com
800-525-5556
Many madeleine pans to choose from, pastry utensils, flavorings, extracts, cake boxes, and more.

## KING ARTHUR FLOUR
www.kingarthurflour.com
800-827-6836
Madeleine pans, large supply of baking equipment, ingredients, treat boxes, gluten-free flour.

## KITCHEN KRAFTS
www.kitchenkrafts.com
800-298-5389
Nonstick madeleine pans, home baking supplies, tools and ingredients, vanilla powder.

## NEILSEN-MASSEY VANILLAS
www.nielsenmassey.com
800-525-7873
Vanilla and other extracts, from pastes to powders to whole beans.

## SUR LA TABLE
www.surlatable.com
800-243-0852
Madeleine pans, wonderful variety of quality baking and cooking utensils, equipment, tabletop and serving ware.

## WILLIAMS-SONOMA
www.williams-sonoma.com
877-812-6235
Madeleine pans, French whisks, quality baking utensils, ingredients, and beautiful serving dishes.

# ❧ METRIC CONVERSIONS ❧

Use these rounded equivalents to convert between the traditional American systems used to measure volume and weight and the metric system.

## VOLUME

| AMERICAN | IMPERIAL | METRIC |
|---|---|---|
| 1/4 teaspoon | | 1.25 milliliters |
| 1/2 teaspoon | | 2.5 milliliters |
| 1 teaspoon | | 5 milliliters |
| 1 tablespoon | | 15 milliliters |
| 1/4 cup (4 tablespoons) | 2 fluid ounces | 60 milliliters |
| 1/3 cup (5 tablespoons) | 2 1/2 fluid ounces | 75 milliliters |
| 1/2 cup (8 tablespoons) | 4 fluid ounces | 125 milliliters |
| 2/3 cup (10 tablespoons) | 5 fluid ounces | 150 milliliters |
| 3/4 cup (12 tablespoons) | 6 fluid ounces | 175 milliliters |
| 1 cup (16 tablespoons) | 8 fluid ounces | 250 milliliters |
| 1 1/4 cups | 10 fluid ounces | 300 milliliters |
| 1 1/2 cups | 12 fluid ounces | 355 milliliters |
| 1 pint (2 cups) | 16 fluid ounces | 500 milliliters |

## WEIGHTS

| AMERICAN | METRIC | AMERICAN | METRIC |
|---|---|---|---|
| 1/4 ounce | 7 grams | 8 ounces (1/2 pound) | 225 grams |
| 1/2 ounce | 15 grams | 9 ounces | 250 grams |
| 1 ounce | 30 grams | 10 ounces | 280 grams |
| 2 ounces | 55 grams | 11 ounces | 310 grams |
| 3 ounces | 85 grams | 12 ounces (3/4 pound) | 340 grams |
| 4 ounces (1/4 pound) | 110 grams | 13 ounces | 370 grams |
| 5 ounces | 140 grams | 14 ounces | 400 grams |
| 6 ounces | 170 grams | 15 ounces | 425 grams |
| 7 ounces | 200 grams | 16 ounces (1 pound) | 450 grams |

# ❧ ACKNOWLEDGMENTS ❧

Thank you to my amazing husband, Matt, and daughter, Laney, for tasting dozens of madeleines with enormous self-sacrifice, patience, and humor. You have had unwavering belief in me, and I love you. To the memory of my parents, Lorraine and Joe, my Nanny Rose, and Uncle Stevie, for instilling a love of good food, prepared well. I miss you all.

To my sister, Harriett, a kindred baking spirit. To my brother Marky, who has always supported my endeavors as long as they were fudge brownies.

To Uncle Alan, Auntie Ruthie, and Auntie Faye for their love and the best cheesecakes and kugel in the galaxy.

To my friends who have offered endless support through the folds and wrinkles of life, for their enthusiasm and encouragement.

To Ben Fieman and Russell Hudson for their willingness to finish every dessert to the last crumb to make absolutely certain it's up to their standards.

To Wannie Tsafos for her love, friendship, and shlepping around San Francisco so I could find the right chocolate.

To France Fortier for her charm, wit, and discerning palate.

To Ellen Peil, Anne McLaughlin, Nancy Gagnon, Steven Griffiths, Jeremy Burrell, and the memory of Donna Driscoll-Tarnoff for great love, kindness, and mostly fun.

To my friends at the Hill Institute, Weavers of Western Mass., and Webs, talented textile artists and madeleine devotees.

To the Kandalafts, friends and owners of Tony's Clam Shop, for supplying me with fried clams for inspiration.

To Paul Wahlberg, chef/owner of Alma Nove, for being enthusiastic about this project and saying the almond madeleines were the best he's ever eaten.

To Julia Child, Maida Heatter, Alice Medrich, Francois Payard, David Lebovitz, Ina Garten, Nick Malgieri, and all the other bakers from whom I have learned so much. To Billy Crystal, Ellen DeGeneres, Robin Williams, Bette Midler, Dave Barry, and too many musicians to name for helping long hours in the kitchen melt away.

To all the many testers and tasters.

To Susan Ginsburg, who first saw the potential for *Madeleines*, for her calm, steady guidance.

To Meghan Rabbitt, for her enthusiasm, professionalism, talent, and invaluable contribution, and for making it fun throughout. Working with Meghan was like catching a wave on the same surfboard, total joy. Thank you! And to Amy Greeman, who led me to Meghan.

To Steve Legato for making madeleines look beautifully delicious. To Mariellen Melker for providing props, styling suggestions, and kind presence. To Amanda Richmond, whose clear vision helped create beautiful, enticing photos. To Tiffany Hill, editor and impromptu baker's assistant. And to the rest of Quirk Books' Team Madeleines!

# ❖INDEX❖

MADELEINES

MADELEINES

INDEX

# ❖ ABOUT THE AUTHOR ❖

BARBARA FELDMAN MORSE IS AN AWARD-WINNING BAKER AND recipe developer. She baked for films, Ted Williams, and Vermont governor Madeleine Kunin while owning and operating her baking business "Cocoa Beans." She is a master weaver and a Nantucket basket maker, and she loves flower gardening, dogs, all kinds of music, and chocolate. She lives in Amherst, Massachusetts, with her husband, daughter, pug Rosie, and furry pup Kiwi. Visit Barbara at www.enjoymadeleines.com.